TRACKING THOSE INCREDIBLE DINOSAURS

. . . and the People Who Knew Them

by

John D. Morris, Ph.D.

CLP C·L·P PUBLISHERS

Tracking Those Incredible Dinosaurs
. . . and the People Who Knew Them

Copyright © 1980

CLP Publishers
P. O. Box 15666
San Diego, California 92115

Library of Congress Catalog Card Number 80-67760
ISBN 0-89051-067-9

Cataloging in Publication Data

Morris, John David, 1946 -
    Tracking those incredible dinosaurs: and the people who knew them.
1. Paluxy River site. 2. Dinosauria. 3. Paleontology—Cretaceous. I. Title.

917.64   80-67760

ISBN 0-89051-067-9

Printed in the United States of America

Dedicated to the Memory of

Stan Taylor

and

Mike Turnage

Acknowledgments

Although this book has only one author, it records the efforts, writings, ideas, photographs, interviews, etc. of many others. Unfortunately, most of these dedicated people must remain unnamed. But certain ones have contributed in especially significant ways, and they must be not only acknowledged, but heartily thanked. All have sought to do their work unselfishly and carefully, convinced they were doing it to the glory of God.

The greatest contributions came from two dear friends, who, since their recent deaths, have now gained a fuller understanding of the events and evidence discussed in the following chapters. Both Stan Taylor and Mike Turnage are now with the One Who is the Source of all knowledge.

The families of these two stalwart investigators have been most gracious in providing any and all information requested. Mrs. Marian Taylor and son Paul Taylor have extended the ministry of Stan Taylor by opening their files and minds for this research and by proofreading and correcting the manuscript when necessary, as well as supplying numerous photographs. Likewise, Mrs. Jean Turnage cooperated in every possible way to see her husband's valuable work vindicated and published.

Other names come to mind that must be acknowledged. Tom Henderson worked with this author both on the site and elsewhere, providing material and wise counsel. Much the same could be said for Clifford Burdick, Wilbur Fields, Cecil Dougherty, and Fred Beierle—all veteran researchers and all of whom have written on this subject. All were more than willing to aid in this composite work. Steve Austin, Fernando Guilarte, Dale Murphy, Walter DiPietro, George Westcott, Marvin Herrman, and many, many others played significant roles in compiling, critiquing, or publishing this research.

A special word of thanks also goes to my father, Dr. Henry M. Morris, from whom I have inherited an interest in and dedication to creation-oriented research. Without his original thinking and writings of the past decades, neither this research nor the publishing of it would have been possible; and without his strong, but quiet leadership and example, his son would not have chosen such a rewarding vocation.

About
The Author

John Morris is well known for his interest in both the geological and archaeological aspects of the Flood of Noah. He has been communicating his research by means of books, lectures, and radio and television appearances ever since his first trip to Mt. Ararat in 1971. His books include *Adventure on Ararat* (1973) and *The Ark on Ararat* (1976).

Dr. Morris received his Ph.D. in Geological Engineering from the University of Oklahoma in 1980. He previously received his M.S. in Geological Engineering at the University of Oklahoma in 1977, and his B.S. in Civil Engineering at Virginia Tech in 1969. He served three years as an engineer with the city of Los Angeles and three years as field scientist with the Institute for Creation Research in San Diego. He has also served as research assistant and instructor in geological engineering at the University of Oklahoma and as a Visiting Lecturer in Geology at Hillsdale Baptist College and Christian Heritage College.

Contents

Contents

Chapter 1

The Controversy

It has been over a hundred years since Charles Darwin wrote his famous book *Origin of Species,* which, more than any other single event, brought the concept of evolution by natural selection to the forefront Within a generation or so, nearly every scientist had accepted the concept, but it was not until the famous Scopes Trial in 1925 that most of the *vocal* opposition to evolution was silenced. Even though a nominal victory was scored by the fundamentalists, the creationist viewpoint was ridiculed by the press and in academic circles. For nearly four decades this situation became progressively worse, with the scientific and educational establishments either ignoring or ridiculing any vestiges of scientific creationism.

This is not the case at the present time, however. In 1961 a controversial but significant book was published that documented many scientific evidences which seemed incompatible with the evolutionary uniformitarian concept. This book, *The Genesis Flood,*[1] by Drs. Henry M. Morris and John C. Whitcomb, presented an apparently credible scientific case for Biblical creationism and Flood geology, while thoroughly refuting uniformitarian geology, and soon pre-

These two human-like and the single dinosaurian footprints appeared in the book The Genesis Flood *by Whitcomb and Morris. While some have questioned the origin of the prints, they did call attention to the Paluxy River, and research began soon after.*

cipitated a revival of both scientific and philosophic interest in the subject. Today the scientific creation movement is alive and well, with many thousands of laymen and scientists involved, and the number is growing rapidly.

One of the most interesting and controversial sections of *The Genesis Flood* dealt with anomalous fossils[2] (fossils that do not seem to fit the assumed evolutionary scheme). Probably the most interesting example was that of the reported discovery of both human and dinosaur tracks in Cretaceous (dinosaur age) strata near Glen Rose, Texas.

Human and dinosaur tracks found together—fossilized in the same layer of limestone! The significance of such a situation is great indeed. If genuine, it could only mean that man and dinosaur lived at the same time and in the same place. According to the evolutionary timetable, dinosaurs are supposed to have lived from about 225 million years ago until they all died out about 70 million years ago. But man (according to the theory) evolved only about one to five million years ago.

Obviously, there should be a long gap of about 65 million years between the extinction of dinosaurs and the appearance of mankind. No consistent evolutionist would claim that man and dinosaur lived together —despite what we read in the comic strips and see on Saturday morning cartoon shows. If the theory is correct, no evidence should exist to the contrary. But the pictures and discussions in *The Genesis Flood* indicated otherwise, as does the information gathered at Glen Rose subsequent to the book's publication.

Most scientists and scholars have chosen to ignore the evidence, while others, such as Dr. A. E. Wilder-Smith realize that:

> If it could be conclusively proved that mod-

ern man had lived at the same time as the giant saurians, scientists would be forced to rethink the whole presently accepted evolutionary Darwinistic concept. One well-documented factual observation of this sort would rob the theory of the huge time spans regarded as a *conditio sine qua non* for evolution to have occurred.

On this basis it would be simply impossible for an evolutionist to imagine a modern man living contemporaneously with the giant lizards. One London biologist, when this possibility was discussed in his presence [of man tracks and brontosaurus tracks having been found in the same formation], remarked that a single such find would provide sound reason for renouncing all evolutionary theory. He was a convinced evolutionist.[3]

The purpose of this book is to provide such evidence. All information from the Glen Rose area that is pertinent to the subject will be provided. It is the author's opinion that the evidence is extensive and that it demands the conclusion that man and dinosaur walked at the *same time* and in the *same place.* Others, using the same evidence, have not come to that conclusion, and, in fairness, their arguments will be presented as well. But the main thrust of this book will be to document the evidence and to place all worthwhile information in one place—with the goal of encouraging those who are so inclined to accept it, confronting those who are not, and to provide all with a comprehensive and definitive reference tool.

References for Chapter 1

1. Morris, Henry M., and Whitcomb, John C., *The Genesis Flood,* Nutley, NJ: Presbyterian and Reformed Publishing Co., 1961.
2. *Ibid.,* pp. 172-176.
3. Wilder-Smith, A. E., *Man's Origin, Man's Destiny,* Wheaton, IL: Harold Shaw Co., 1974, pp. 293-294.

Chapter 2

History of the Find

If human tracks do exist in the same strata as dinosaur tracks, the basic assumption of evolution (that of long ages of evolutionary development) is violated. Since this find is so important, it has enjoyed a great deal of publicity among creationists. On the other hand, those evolutionists who have acknowledged the data have, of course, tried to find some explanation which would not require admitting that man and dinosaur were contemporaries.

Current interest developed primarily out of work begun in the late 1960's. Until then the discovery suffered in relative obscurity, and even now controversy swirls around attempts to reconstruct those early days.

The Paluxy River is a paradox in itself. At normal water levels it sparkles calmly downstream on its way to the nearby Brazos River. Occasionally, it completely dries up, but at flood stage it becomes a raging torrent. It drops an average of 17 feet per mile and, as such, is the second swiftest river in Texas.

The river floods less frequently now since flood control has been instituted upstream, but the local residents vividly describe the power of the Paluxy during a

In May 1979 the usually calm Paluxy was transformed into a raging torrent, and water levels, usually less than 2', rose to 30'.

Photo by Berry

The Paluxy River at normal water level.

Aftermath of May, 1979, flood. Debris caught in trees and farm lands area-wide. In this picture, the water level has receded, but is still about 3' above normal.

flood. The rising waters have flooded the town many times and have damaged farms and farm houses over and over again. They say the noise of the rushing waters is completely drowned out by the frightening sound of boulders and rock shelves, weighing up to several tons, being washed downstream by the water's fury—colliding, grinding, and breaking as they go.

One of the worst floods on record ransacked the generally flat countryside in 1908 when the river rose 27 feet, ' and it was after this flood that the controversial footprints were first noted. The erosion of a clay layer in one area revealed tracks, some of which appeared to be human and others which appeared to be dinosaur, and the removal of an entire shelf in another area exposed even more. Soon numerous similar tracks were discovered throughout the area. Most were dinosaur tracks of one sort or another, but some looked man-like.

Trail of three-toed dinosaur footprints. © *Films for Christ, Photo by P. Taylor.*

Charlie Moss, long-time Glen Rose resident and footprint enthusiast, discovered both human and dinosaur tracks.

Perhaps the clearest man-like trail was discovered by Ernest "Bull" Adams in 1908, who showed the tracks to Charlie Moss, Zollie Wilkens, Roy Garner, and others. Moss is still alive and has been most helpful in the exploration work. On December 19, 1950, he signed the following statement detailing the trail of prints in response to the investigation of Dr. Clifford Burdick, a geologist from Tucson, Arizona:

> This is to certify that I, Charles Moss, of Glen Rose, Texas, saw and inspected, from about 1908 to 1918, on the north bank of the Paluxy River, six miles north of Glen Rose, Texas, one quarter mile west of the ford on the river, about 15 tracks or footprints of apparent giant human beings. The tracks measured about 18 inches from heel to toe, the five toes being plainly marked. The first few tracks were about 6 feet apart; then from 8 to 10 feet apart as the person started to run. In these prints only the toes and balls of the feet were

in evidence. They were in an 8-inch layer of limestone along the river bank.

About 1918 a flood came on the river and excavated and carried away all the strata with the footprints. Downstream later could be seen fragments of rock slabs turned upside down in the stream. It is possible that with proper power machinery these slabs could be turned over and new footprints found: or the bank at the bend of the river could be excavated. (Glen Rose, Texas, December 19, 1950.)

Mr. Moss, who has spent many years looking into the subject, still tells his story to the curious. "The tracks were clear. I remember how the skin between the little toe and the one next to it had grown together

Bandstand in Glen Rose, Texas, has this print exhibited.

on the right foot.'' But the prints are gone now. When asked if he had ever taken a picture of the prints, Mr. Moss reported that he had not, but remembered that all of the local residents felt that such footprints must have been common throughout the world. Indeed, they were common in Glen Rose, and few of the residents had traveled anywhere else.

In the early 1920's, in the height of the Great Depression, residents of this hard-hit area had to rely on their resourcefulness to make ends meet. It was found that the prints had economic value when removed from the water. A good dinosaur track would bring up to fifty dollars, although man tracks were not so valuable. Over the next few years several dozen dino-

Hole in the riverbed where Jim and Cecil Ryals claim to have removed an excellent human print.

saur tracks were removed, as well as a smaller number of human tracks.

One such enterprise was carried out by James and Cecil Ryals who, because they found it difficult to feed their family of eight children, began to quarry the prints. After the farm work was done for the day, they would go down to the river to excavate fossil tracks. He would hold the long chisel made from the axle of a discarded Model-T Ford while she would swing the eight-pound sledge hammer. Depending on the hardness of the rock, the job would take from a few hours to a week.[2]

In order to preserve the details of the print, and to lessen the possibility of cracking the rock, a wide circle was cut around the track, sometimes ruining the preceding and following tracks. At times a metal strip was placed around the slab to strengthen it as it was torqued out of its place and carried away.

Ryals, who was by far the most active resident engaged in the removal of the prints, estimates that over the years he quarried about 100 dinosaur tracks, but only about 10 human tracks. He also remembered removing what looked to him to be an elephant track, although it must be acknowledged that the front feet of some sauropods were of similar shape.

Ryals and the others tell how common it was to find both man and dinosaur tracks together. In fact a large slab containing good prints of both just a few inches apart was removed in 1934. The whereabouts of the track are not known now, but the 4' x 5' pothole is still conspicuous.

It was these prints, removed from the river and sold to various individuals, that first called attention to the area. In the fall of 1938, Roland T. Bird, a paleontologist employed by the American Museum of Natural History in New York City chanced to see two human-

like tracks and two dinosaur tracks in an Indian tra-
der's store in Gallup, New Mexico. In his most interesting article he relates his initial reaction to the human-like tracks.

> It seemed too good to believe any living crea-
> ture had made prints like that to turn up here
> unnoticed and unsung in a trader's store . . . .
> For a moment I had them to myself—the
> strangest things of their kind I had ever seen.
> On the surface of each was splayed the near-
> likeness of a human foot, perfect in every de-
> tail. But each imprint was 15 inches long! . . .
> I could conceive of no animal that might have
> made them. It was ridiculous to think they
> were human footprints. They were too large
> and bear-like; and yet they weren't like the
> largest prehistoric bear I could think of, the
> great Pleistocene cave bear, for the toes were
> not typical.[3]

Bird concluded that the prints were carvings, not
true footprints. However, his interest was heightened
by the information that the tracks were found in the
same stratigraphic layer as dinosaur tracks, and that
the owner, a Mr. Jack Hill, owned several of them too.

> The dinosaur footprints were found as rep-
> resented and, like the "mystery tracks," they
> were fine specimens—too fine. I had every
> reason to suspect the entire lot had been fash-
> ioned by some stone artist, but how they had
> been so neatly done, how a man could have
> duplicated the dinosaur track, at least, without
> an intimate knowledge of something genuine,
> there was no means of telling . . . . If the
> dinosaur tracks were genuine, could the strange
> prints be those of some hitherto unknown rep-
> tile?[4]

The trail of Brontosaur tracks found by Moss, Adams, and others in the early twenties was removed by Roland Bird.   *Photo by Moss.*

And, so, on a hunch, Mr. Bird traveled to Glen Rose. While in Glen Rose, Mr. Bird documented many exposed dinosaur trails, including the trail of a sauropod (the group of huge dinosaurs that includes the well-known brontosaur). Until that time no such trail had been documented in scientific circles, but many residents of Glen Rose had known of this one and others for years. Wayland Adams has boyhood memories of playing in the tracks on family picnics in the early twenties. Charlie Moss took pictures of them in 1934. But as it turns out, the credit for the discovery of such remarkable finds went instead to Roland Bird. Eventually, the trail was removed from the river bed and placed on permanent display at the Museum of Natural History in New York, just to the rear of the brontosaur skeleton, and made to look as if the animal had just walked there. Additional prints were excavated by the University of Texas at Austin, where they are now shown in a similar display.

In order to investigate the human-like tracks, Bird sought help from local residents. For example, Charlie Moss, who had led him to the sauropod trail, was thoroughly rebuked for referring to them as human tracks because "man had not yet evolved at the time of the dinosaurs. They must have been made by some sort of ape."[5] This off-the-cuff remark does not solve anything, however, because—according to evolution—apes preceded man by only a few million years. *Apes* and dinosaurs together would be almost as damaging to evolution as *men* and dinosaurs together. Mr. Bird told Mrs. Elsie McFall that if he were to acknowledge the presence of man tracks in Cretaceous strata, all the textbooks would have to be rewritten.[6]

James Ryals, who had excavated so many tracks, was asked about the "mystery prints":

> Much to my surprise he said, "Oh, you mean the man tracks. Why, sure, there used to be a whole trail of them up above the fourth crossing, before the river washed them out."
>
> My surprise was partly overcome by Ryals' casual reference to them as human footprints. I smiled. No man had existed in the Age of

Reptiles . . . . I asked, "Can you show me one?" . . . I watched closely as the outline of a foot took form, something about 15 inches long with a curious elongated heel. What I saw was discouraging in one sense, enlightening in another. Apparently it had been made by some hitherto unknown dinosaur or reptile. The original mud had been very soft at this point, and the rock had preserved faithfully this element of softness, but the track lacked definition on which to base conclusions. There was only the one, and though my eyes itched to see a good one, the overlying ledge covered any possible next print.[7]

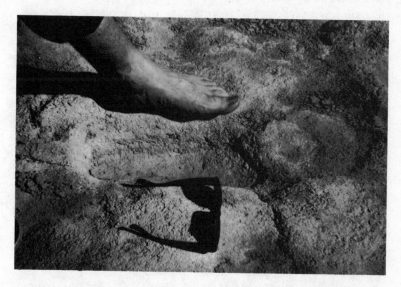

Roland Bird described the "mystery print" shown to him by Jim Ryals as having a "curious elongated heel," and felt that it must have been made by some "hitherto unknown dinosaur."   *Photo by Taylor.*

Upright Tyrannosaurus Rex model (left) and foot (above). Most of the dinosaur prints in the Paluxy River are of this basic type, although from several species.

The huge Brontosaurus (above) and foot (left). The first discovery of this type dinosaur footprint was in the Paluxy.

In all the rest of his writings, Mr. Bird made only passing comments to the man-like tracks, and then only wondering what kind of unknown reptile could have made them. Years later, Ryals commented that he never could understand this man's attitude of "completely ignoring the man tracks while at the same time being so enthusiastic about dinosaur tracks. Nature placed both kinds there and they both deserved study."[8]

Bird was careful to state his conviction that man and dinosaur could not have coexisted and, therefore, that the elongated tracks could not have been made by humans. But while his insistence is noted, it is also true that a cloud of mystery still hangs over much of the work that he did. Many questions remain to be answered, even about his excavation site. Wayland "Slim" Adams (son of Ernest "Bull" Adams who aided Bird in his work), distinctly remembers a trail of human tracks running diagonally across the river, crossing the upriver end of Bird's sandbagged excavation. According to him and others who corroborate the story,[9] the prints were unmistakably human, especially when freshly exposed.

A recent booklet published by Theodore Schreiber, a protege' of Roland Bird, quotes extensively from articles, notes, and letters written by the late Bird himself, and provides a sketch of the excavation site drawn by Bird at the time.[10] A close look at this previously unpublished sketch shows a series of three elongated markings running diagonally across the upriver end of the sandbagged area. Two of these were removed, one by the American Museum and the other by the University of Texas. The museum specimen is labeled only as "Single Giant Track," with no reference to the others in the legend. In a subsequent letter Schreiber insisted that "R. T. Bird's reference to the A. M. Single Giant

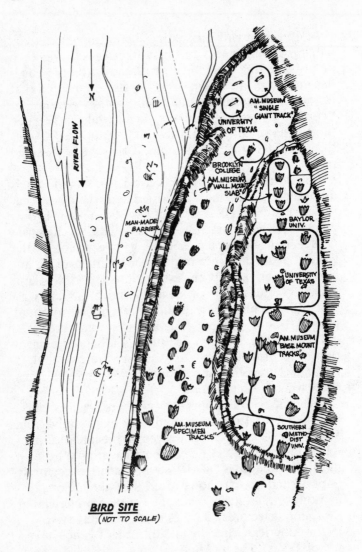

BIRD SITE
(NOT TO SCALE)

This drawing is from Bird's sketch of his work in the Paluxy, showing the locations and contents of the slabs of rock removed for display elsewhere. Note the unexplained reference to the removal of a "single giant track."

Track referred only to the one giant sauropod track."[1] Copies of Bird's photos on file at the University of Texas at Austin have been studied by Mike Turnage, but none of the upriver end of the excavation was available. It would be interesting to study the remainder of Bird's photos, as it would to know what became of the two removed "giant tracks." Until answers to those questions are forthcoming, the cloud of mystery remains.

When Bird's article appeared in 1939, it came to the attention of the creationist scientists associated with The Society for the Study of Creation, the Deluge, and Related Sciences of Los Angeles. In the early 1940's, a committee of five was appointed to investigate. One of these men, Dr. Clifford Burdick, followed through. His investigations first led him to Mr. Al Berry, operator of a roadside museum on Highway 66 near Sanders, Arizona, who owned several specimens.

In 1938, Mr. Berry had heard from a friend about the possibility of man and dinosaur tracks together near Glen Rose, but was alarmed that construction in the river bed was likely to mar or destroy them; so, he and Jack Hill (the owner of the prints that Roland Bird was to see later) journeyed to Texas to investigate. Mr. Berry has now passed away, but before he died he signed the following affidavit:

> It was in the year 1938, the month of September, I believe, that Jack Hill from Palestine, Texas, and I made the trip to the Paluxy River, near Glen Rose, Texas. In the river bed, in what we believe was limestone, we found many dinosaur tracks, several saber-toothed tiger tracks, and three human tracks. There was a man working at the dam which was under construction who had dug up ten or more

tracks which he was keeping [sic]. Jack and I hired this jackhammer operator to break loose two saber-toothed tiger tracks, two dinosaur tracks, and two human tracks.

Mr. Hill took the saber-toothed tiger tracks with him. The last I saw of these was at the Three Hogans Trading Post, west of Gallup, New Mexico, I believe about 1939 or 1940. The human and dinosaur tracks are now at the Glen City Rock Shop, and belong to me. This is the full story which I certify to be true.

> Signed: Allen J. Berry
> Notarized: August 25, 1965
> Farmington, New Mexico

The tracks have since been sold to Columbia Union College of Takoma Park, Maryland; but despite this affidavit as to their authenticity, subsequent tests run on the tracks have cast some doubts. This subject will be discussed fully in Chapter 7, but for now, suffice it to say that these prints caught the attention of Dr. Burdick and launched the study of the Glen Rose area by creationist scientists, an investigation that continues now with as much fervor as ever.

Dr. Burdick's sporadic trips to Glen Rose over the following forty years resulted in several widely-read articles,[12] and his material was used by others in books, including *The Genesis Flood* by Drs. John C. Whitcomb and Henry M. Morris, and *Man's Origin, Man's Destiny* by A. E. Wilder-Smith. These publications continued to increase the interest in the subject.

References for Chapter 2

1. Bierle, Fredrick P., *Man, Dinosaurs, and History,* Prosser, Washington: Perfect Printing, 1977, p. 17.
2. Westcott, George W., "Fossil Tracks in the Paluxy River Bed," (unpublished manuscript), p. 7.
3. Bird, Roland T., "Thunder in His Footsteps," *Natural History,* May, 1938, p. 255.
4. *Ibid.,* pp. 255-256.
5. Westcott, p. 7.
6. *Ibid.*
7. Bird, p. 257.
8. Westcott, p. 9.
9. Beierle, p. 28.
10. Schreiber, V. Theodore, *Dinosaur Valley State Park: Where the Big Ones Ate and Ran,* Shirleysburg, PA, 1978.
11. Personal correspondence, September 14, 1979.
12. Burdick, "Footprints in the Sands of Time," *Creation Research Society Quarterly,* V. 2, December, 1974, p. 164.

Chapter 3

Footprints in Stone

In the mid 1960's news of Dr. Clifford Burdick's work reached Mr. Stanley Taylor, then Director of Films for Christ Association, Elmwood, Illinois, through the book *The Genesis Flood*. As his interest grew, Taylor decided to include a brief documentation of the footprints in a proposed dramatic film entitled *Trail From Eden,* which was to focus on the current creation-evolution controversy. In 1968 he took his crew to Glen Rose to meet with Dr. Burdick and film the supposed footprints.

What he and the others found, however, so captivated them that a second movie was born, which was to document exclusively the presence of man and dinosaur tracks together. The film, *Footprints in Stone,* released in January, 1973, has been widely circulated, but the story of its development and the controversy which has swirled around it is equally fascinating.

Almost all information concerning human tracks from the Paluxy that had been circulated by this time centered around specimens that had been seen in New Mexico by Roland Bird, Clifford Burdick, and others: two tracks on display, one at the Gibbs Sanitarium in Glen Rose, and the other at Dr. C. C. Cook's office

Stanley E. Taylor, director of Films for Christ.

Dr. Burdick points out the location of a print found by digging down through the bank. The print is part of a trail of three large tracks.
© *Films for Christ.*

in Cleburne, Texas, and another track which Dr. Burdick had purchased. All of these, of course, had been supposedly removed from the river, and there was some dispute about their origin. Aside from a few mediocre possibilities in the river bed that Dr. Burdick had investigated, these constituted at that time the main evidence that man and dinosaur had lived concurrently.

The problem of carved tracks will be discussed fully in Chapter 9, and it is quite a problem, as Taylor found out. While much of his careful research indicated that some, if not all, of these prints were carvings, his enthusiasm was sustained by reports that the carvings were copies of original prints as found in the river.

After hearing Charlie Moss' statement concerning the trail of human prints which had been washed away in 1918, Taylor hired a local contractor to help explore the downstream bend in the river in hopes that the slab containing the prints had been deposited there. For two days a bulldozer dug and moved slabs, overturning many, but no prints of any sort were found.

In a few places scattered around the area, elongated features that might have been eroded human tracks were seen in the river bottom, leading shoreward. Several of these were investigated, but all but one proved unfruitful, and even that one proved inconclusive. The trail consists of large moccasin-shaped prints, each of which had a contour compatible with that of a human foot, but the prints were each 16 inches long with a stride of about 70 inches. The first track was plainly visible in the river and the second was partially covered by the west bank of the river. By measuring the direction and stride, Taylor and his crew predicted the location of the next print and found it by digging down through the bank. Unfortunately, no

detailed features were visible since the mud must have
been very soft at the time the prints were made (now,
of course, it has turned to stone). The prints actually
penetrated through the six-inch layer of limestone into
the clay layer below. Potential benefits of exploring
for a possible fourth print in the series were oversha-
dowed by the difficulties of excavation and the inconclusive nature of the prints.

The Films for Christ investigators then moved to an
area between the McFall and Kerr farms where many
Glen Rose residents had reported seeing a number of
human trails. In a special release Taylor reported:

> Guided by Emmet McFall and his son, Ja-
> cob, we were first shown a row of giant moc-
> casin tracks very near the McFall shore. In the
> midst of these they pointed out a large circular
> hole where one of the moccasin tracks had
> been dug out along with a dinosaur track. The
> McFalls were not able to tell us where it had
> been sold, but recalled that a man named Jim
> Ryals had dug it out back in the 30's. Next,
> they took us downstream to a trail of eroded
> giant barefoot tracks. On one we could still see
> the impression left by the big toe and the gen-
> eral shape of the rest of the foot. In the middle
> of this trail we also noted a large circular hole.
> They told us that here again Jim Ryals, back in
> the 30's, had dug out a perfect barefoot giant
> human track.

> Jacob McFall then took us to an area (it was
> now covered with sand and rock) where he, as
> a youth, had dug out a barefoot man track in
> the early 30's. He believed if we brought in
> heavy equipment we could dig down to the ex-
> act location. As he recalled, there were several
> footprints leading to the hole where he had

Part of what is now known as the Ryals trail (left). Here Jim Ryals removed a "perfect" human footprint. The hole remains "in stride" with other prints in the trail.

© Films for Christ.

Removing overhanging ledges in several places (below) exposed new prints.

Jim Ryals and his wife Cecil (bottom) removed a "perfect" human track from this location. Here they tell John Read and the filming crew the details while Jacob McFall listens. © Films for Christ.

removed the track, although he remembered they were not nearly as clear as the one he had removed.

For this work we hired a large rubber-tired caterpillar with a 9-foot scoop. Under the guidance of Jacob McFall we carefully removed the rock and sand from the area. Soon we uncovered the large round hole where he had chiseled out the track. Carefully cleaning away the mud and sand we noted five tracks leading toward the hole. These prints were not as large or deep as others we had seen. In the two tracks leading up to the hole it was easy to make out the general outline of a bare human footprint, the heel, the arch, and the front outline of the foot, although the separation between the toes was not clearly indicated. Jacob told us that the toe prints had been clearly outlined in the track he had dug out. He recalled that this track had broken in two pieces, but that he had been able to sell it to Dr. Cook in Cleburne back in the 30's. Following the line of tracks backward, we noted that in the first prints the man had walked on the ball of his foot and the tracks also became less distinct.

We then moved the Caterpillar upstream about a quarter of a mile to investigate a rock outcropping at the far end of the McFall place almost directly across from the two cottages on the Kerr farm. This was one of the few places where footprints had been seen in a layer of rock other than the riverbed strata. The area was about five feet above the water. Several large man-like tracks had been noted here where the surface rock had been eroded back. They ran parallel to the river and then curved directly away from it. Operating from the river, the scoop operator was able to reach the top outcropping ledge and lift back several large slabs. As a result we uncovered three previously unexposed man-like tracks. It was obvious that the footprints had been made in deep mud and the mud had partially run together as the foot had been withdrawn.

Our final excavation was in an area just below where Jacob McFall had dug out the track to which we have previously referred. Here we uncovered two new tracks which appear to be an extension of a trail of man-like tracks coming diagonally up river. Neither were as clear as we would have wished, although one did show five toe prints. It is to this area that we plan to return for continued investigations. On the return trip we also plan to sandbag and photograph a number of the better underwater tracks.[1]

One final series of tracks was pointed out to Taylor by Mrs. Charlie Moss on a ledge near the extension of the series of Bird's brontosaurus tracks. Here three or four tracks in stride were exposed and were so detailed that Taylor wrote that "anyone with an unbiased mind would accept this as a human footprint."[2]

Returning to the Paluxy in the summer of 1969, the Films for Christ crew was joined by a number of interested helpers, including a group from the Lubbock, Texas Bible Church, led by Pastor Charles Clough. Searching the river bottom in numerous places several new possible trails were discovered but none of a conclusive nature.

The decision had been made the previous year to return to the north bank of the river at the Kerr property in an attempt to follow the trail from which Jacob

McFall had removed a human print.

We decided to attempt to backtrack this individual and sandbag an area of more than 200 feet directly down river. After removing the overhanging rock ledge with the caterpillar scoop, we removed the sand and water with shovels, wheelbarrows, and pumps.

Our first discoveries at the upper end of this newly sandbagged area were a couple of what appeared to be young brontosaurus tracks, then a three-toed dinosaur track, and then what looked like might have been a human footprint freshly damaged by the iron fingers of the caterpillar scoop. Geologist Dr. Clifford Burdick traced an outline of this and described it as appearing to him to be an authentic human footprint showing the toes.

Near the lower end of the excavated area we found a line of 10 more man-like tracks. They appeared to have been eroded by water but certainly did have an elongated man-like shape, with a left and right stride such as a human being would make. Some showed an indication of heel, instep, and ball of the foot. The clearest of them measured nine and one-half inches and fit a 15-year-old boy's foot quite nicely. The last of these tracks led us under a ledge into the riverbank. We decided to follow.

Using two bulldozers we cleared away another hundred feet or so of earth down to the overlying limestone ledge. After examining this limestone ledge, which was about nine inches in depth, and finding only some slightly impressed dinosaur tracks on it, we proceded to tear it out in order to get down to the river strata below. Underneath were about three inches of gravel and then more of the fossil tracks. Picking up our trail again, we found five more man-like footprints. These crossed diagonally a newly uncovered row of 15 three-toed dinosaur tracks. One of these man-like footprints actually stepped onto the edge of a dinosaur track. Two of the tracks showed an outline of what appeared to be the front of a man's toes. The last print showed only what was probably the ball of a foot. Beyond this the stratum dipped into what had perhaps been a pool of water at the time the tracks were made.

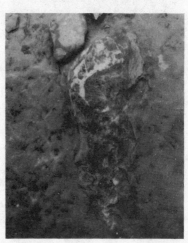

18" track exposed by bull-dozer excavation. The whitish calcite etching on toes is due to the weight of the individual who made the print. Even though the print had been damaged, the calcite provided the key to the shape of the foot which made the print.
Photo by Burdick.

Meanwhile, at this same site, we discovered a larger man track crossing the smaller man and dinosaur tracks at right angles, aiming directly shoreward into the pasture. There were several of these large tracks, but the first was the best. It showed the outline of a heel and

Stan Taylor and Films for Christ work crew preparing an area for filming.
  Photo by Dougherty.

gave indication of the outline of the front of a foot, including the angle from the big toe to the small.

Interestingly enough, this 18-inch track was only 55 feet from where Jim Ryals had dug out the famous 18-inch track which had been on display at Dr. Cook's hospital in Cleburne.[3]

The expedition in 1970 consisted of extending the previous excavation and the filming of it. But in addition, preparations were made to invite numerous Christian geologists to the site, (some of them known uniformitarians) to see if any other interpretation of the data were possible. And on Thanksgiving weekend, 1970, six prominent scientists brought in by FFC, along with numerous others, gathered at the Snyder Sanitarium in Glen Rose to see the films and plaster casts, and to investigate the prints in the river bed.

As might be expected, the reactions to these evidences were rather varied, ranging from firm confidence to emotional opposition. Each of these six scientists was interviewed on film, and their analyses formed an important part of the movie. Their comments on camera have been transcribed and are reproduced below, interspersed at times with personal comments made by the participants to the author (also present at Glen Rose that weekend).

Dr. Douglas Block, professor of geology at Rock Valley College, Rockford, Illinois (a secular college):

The fact that there are a number of them, the fact that they are elongated, the fact that it seems as though this individual was a bipedal individual walking only on two legs does suggest that this problem is certainly at least open to further investigation. Very frankly, if these were not made by man, we do not know what kind of an animal did produce them.

Numerous scientists gathered on Thanksgiving weekend in 1970 to view the tracks. Comments were varied and at times emotional.

© *FFC, Photo by Taylor.*

Dr. Block had not at the time come out in favor of the creationist model, and was not at all sure he wanted to. But impressed by the footprint evidence, he remained to continue the research after the meeting had broken up and the filming was over. Soon he was convinced. On July 12, 1979, he wrote this author:

I have shared the footprint story with many people in my own classes and on the lecture platform, and I do it because I have no doubt that they [the footprints] are completely human.

As for significance: First, I must differ from the film conclusion that the prints refute evolution. I see no direct reference to that topic at all.

What is abundantly clear is that the two types of tracks in the same shale layer wipe out the classically accepted antiquity of the Cretaceous Period, and they unequivocally refute the chronological separation of the Upper Mesozoic [accepted dinosaur age] from the Pleistocene or Upper Cenozoic [the accepted age for *Homo sapiens*].

Now, you may argue that since the timetable is supposedly built on evolutionary presuppositions, what I have said undermines the validity of evolution—and so it does—but, I believe there are other stronger approaches to that problem.

While it is true that the discovery of human and dinosaur tracks together does not fit the evolutionary scheme, the producers of *Footprints in Stone* were wisely careful not to claim that such evidence disproved evolution. While the film pointed out some of the logical fallacies involved in the evolutionary interpretation, no unreasonable conclusions to this effect

Stan Taylor excavated this ledge which revealed two trails of dinosaurs and three human trails.

were actually made in the film, as Dr. Block's recent comments might have implied.

Dr. Harold Slusher, assistant professor of physics at the University of Texas, El Paso, and chairman of the Geoscience Department at Christian Heritage College in San Diego, as well as Research Associate in Geophysics for the Institute for Creation Research, had this to say:

> I think they are made by man. The geo-metrical arrangement of them seems to indi-cate a man striding across a mud bank. Some of them show very good detail in regard to toes, the instep, and the general shape of the foot. Here and there are prints that seem to have been made by someone wearing mocca-sins or something of that nature. As best I can tell, these tracks seem to be human.

Dr. Slusher, a long-time creationist, has returned to

the Paluxy at times since then and is now more convinced than ever that the prints are of human origin.

Dr. Clifford Burdick, consulting geologist in Tucson:

Although erosion has removed the detail of
the toes, there is still enough to show the shape
of a foot, especially when we put a human foot
in the track—it seems to fit so perfectly . . . to
me the picture becomes more and more complete and more convincing all the time. There
are tracks there which could be called human
without stretching too much of a point.

Dr. Burdick is, of course, a pioneer investigator of
the tracks and has been long convinced of their source.
But this evidence has been under attack not only by
evolutionists, but also by a few creationists who have
refrained from supporting the work. Burdick later
wrote in a letter dated July 20, 1973:

It disgusts me the way so-called creationists
haggle and carp over some real evidence that
could go a long way toward refuting evolutionary geology. When evolutionists come up with
a new theory they don't hesitate to break into
print, although their so-called evidence is not
one-tenth as compelling as this.

Dr. Paul Wright, professor emeritus of geology at
Wheaton College:

It seems to me it had to be made by an animal of some kind. Now as to whether that
animal is human or not: if we look at some
individual tracks you can see some of them
where there is a good mark of the heel, the instep, and some places there are indentations
which could well be toes, but always the angle
comes right back, just at the angle from the big
toe back to the small one. There will be rights
and lefts—and again the heel, the instep, and

the angle from the toes. If it weren't that this is Cretaceous in the table [i.e., Cretaceous Age, ed.] in the limestone, I don't think there would be any question but what these are human footprints. But since they are out of place according to the geologic timetable, then there gets to be considerable question. Are they really and truly human footprints? I'm not ready to say I'm positive they are, but there are so many, and again as I say, in line. They have to have been made by some organism, I believe. And they well could be human footprints. In fact, I wouldn't be a bit surprised if there is more digging and it might finally be authenticated they are real human footprints.

The first time Dr. Wright saw the movie *Footprints in Stone* (which included the above segment) was in August, 1974, in Oklahoma City, at a meeting of the American Scientific Affiliation. (The ASA is a Chris-

Stan Taylor, producer of Footprints in Stone, *was the first to do major excavation in the Paluxy to attempt to find human footprints. He and co-worker Marvin Hermann are shown pointing out a human trail. Photo by Stan Taylor.*

tian organization of scientists which has long been dominated by the concept of theistic evolution, or variations of it.) Taking the stand after the movie, Dr. Wright accused the producers of the movie of misrepresenting him by removing from his original quote his feelings that the find of probable human footprints in the same strata with dinosaur prints did not disprove evolution but would only force a revision of a small part of the geologic timetable. Dr. Wright has always disagreed with the standard theory of evolution in his belief that man is not a descendant of animals, while retaining a modified concept of long ages. Nevertheless, like Dr. Block, he did not wish to appear as though he supported the thrust of the movie. On the contrary, he insisted that the movie be altered.

In the flurry of confrontations that followed, much harm was done to the reputation of the Films for Christ Association, although transcripts and tape recordings of the original interview showed that the quotation in question had not been altered and that Dr. Wright had included no such disclaimer. Such a disclaimer was personally spoken to this author by Dr. Wright the evening the interviews were filmed, but the comment was not made in front of the camera, and in the end, Dr. Wright agreed that his charge of fraud had not been correct.

Dr. Gerald H. Haddock, professor of geology at Wheaton College:

> Some of the people say they see toe marks on them. I do see erosion marks and some of these marks may be an original impression in the sediment. I am not at all convinced that these tracks, which are considerably weathered, are sufficiently intact to say that these are toe marks or moccasin prints as some others have said. I just don't see a clear case for

establishing these definitely as human footprints, and so I think I'll have to go on record
as saying I doubt the allegation very strongly.

Dr. Haddock has been long committed to an old age
for the earth and the general theory of "progressive
creation." In several lengthy conversations with the
author, he repeatedly offered statements such as:

The prints look like man-prints. If they
were in strata designated as recent, they would
be accepted as human. But these tracks are
found in Cretaceous strata, dinosaur age strata, and everybody knows that man and dinosaur didn't live together. These tracks therefore must have been made by some kind of
dinosaur, which we haven't discovered yet,
that had a foot that looked like a man's.

Dr. Henry M. Morris, hydrologist, Director of the
Institute for Creation Research:

These prints, in many cases, are eroded.
Of course, it doesn't take long once a track is
exposed before it becomes almost unrecognizable, just a few years. But at the same time
there are still many that are quite good, both
dinosaur tracks and what appear to be human
tracks. As a matter of fact, we know of no
type of animal, past or present, that could
have made these tracks other than man. And
there is no clear reason why man couldn't have
made them. We could say, for example, that
if they had been found it some more recent
formation, there would be no question that
they were human tracks. The main reason why
some have doubted they are really man tracks
is because it doesn't fit in with the accepted
system. The dinosaur is supposed to have died
out about 100 million years ago or so and man

only appeared about a million years ago. So
the evolutionary chronology and system
doesn't square with the assumption that man
and dinosaur lived at the same time. We feel
that it is the system itself, the evolutionary
uniformitarianism system of chronology, that
needs to be brought under real scrutiny.

Since the release of the movie in 1971, it has been
shown many hundreds of times before audiences of
many kinds and a slightly secularized version has been
shown in public schools and meetings. Its effect has
been incalculable. Many have been exposed to a
strong case for Christianity and the reasonableness of
the Christian faith through the movie. As noted in
Chapter 1, the creation movement has blossomed in
recent years, and no doubt this film has played an important part.

References for Chapter 3

1. Taylor, Stanley E., "Search for Man Tracks in the Paluxy River," Special Report, distributed by Films for Christ, October, 1968.
2. *Ibid.*
3. Taylor, Stanley E., "The Mystery Tracks in Dinosaur Valley," *Bible-Science Newsletter,* V. 9, No. 4, April, 1971, pp. 5, 6.

Chapter 4

Recent Investigations

Taking up where Stan Taylor and Films for Christ left off, were several investigators whose extension of the original work continued to strengthen the case for the presence of human footprints in the Paluxy River bed. The work of each of these individuals or organizations will be discussed briefly, but the most productive and capable was a biologist from Houston, Texas, named Mike Turnage.

Here Mike Turnage is demonstrating the stride between two of the prints in the Turnage trail.

Turnage had been with Taylor on two occasions in Glen Rose, including the interviews with the group of geologists from around the country, and was thoroughly familiar with locations of tracks and with the local residents.

Most of his work in 1971 was spent extending the various man trails at the same site where Taylor had done much of his work. Of the three trails uncovered, one revealed 25 large prints, another 6 giant prints, and the third 8 normal prints, of which several were quite well preserved. Turnage centered most of his attention on this third trail, digging back into the bank.[1]

In June of 1972, he returned with several helpers including scientists Tom Henderson and James Ware. Together they scoured the river for any possible man tracks, making note of any promising markings. They did locate a series of impressions about 200 yards downstream from the Taylor site and proceeded to excavate.

The prints went under a thick pile of gravel on the west bank of the river, evidently a point bar indicating the previous location of the river. Dropping a six-foot square pit down through the gravel revealed that the print layer was highly eroded, and no more prints were found. Next, sandbagging as best they could, they dug back into the bank, only to find that indeed the rock sloughed off and only a total of six prints were found.

The first two prints of this sequence showed some detail, but not enough to make a certain identification. In an effort to establish the origin of the prints, they tried an ingenious method. After consulting with the local sheriff's office on the art of fingerprinting, they closely studied the prints with colored dye and a magnifying glass to see if any toe "fingerprints" remained. Unfortunately, the prints were too eroded to

reveal anything, but this method should be tried elsewhere. After concluding that the series of six tracks
could not be identified, Turnage and the others abandoned them and refused to consider them as evidence.[2,3]

Meanwhile, Cecil Dougherty, a Glen Rose chiropractor, also began to take an active interest. His almost total fascination with the "giant tracks," however, had brought the disapproval of both Taylor and
Turnage.

Dougherty, until his retirement in 1978, had one ad-
vantage no other investigator had, that of living in the
area and being able to spend a great deal of time in the
river, especially when it was dry. For several years he
wandered up and down the river with a broom in
hand, sweeping the bottom of the river and locating
any man-like tracks. As the name of his booklet, *Valley of the Giants,*[4] would imply, his strong interest in
the giant tracks may have kept him from total objec-

*Cecil Dougherty at work on
the "Dougherty site." Note
dinosaur trail starting at bottom.*

tivity, so that much of his work has received criticism
—even from other researchers who are convinced that
some of the Paluxy tracks are human.

Dougherty would readily admit, as he has to the
author on several occasions, that many of the "tracks"
he has located are marginal at best and should not be
used by themselves as proof of the coexistence of giant
men and dinosaurs. Only as the total picture is viewed
do his possible prints take on significance. Some of
those that he likes to feature, such as those on the
cover of the latest editions of his booklet, are some of
the best in the area, and most investigators agree that
that they are human.

The Institute for Creation Research (ICR) had partially financed the work of Mike Turnage in 1971 and
1972, and Drs. Henry Morris, Harold Slusher, Steven

*In 1976 ICR sponsored an investigation with over 50 volunteer workers.
Unfortunately a flash flood left the water deep and muddy.*

Austin, and the author had in one way or another participated in the later stages of the filmings of *Footprints in Stone,* but until 1975 no ICR employee had done any actual personal investigation of the Paluxy. At the invitation of Dr. Dougherty, during August, 1975, Dr. Harold Slusher, Dr. Clifford Burdick, and Dr. Omar Hamara, viewed most of Dougherty's and Burdick's research. Simply by following some of Dougherty's tracks into the river, they were able to discover some new tracks which were quite well preserved.

Again, during October, 1975, the author and Dr. Ed Blick (ICR Advisory Board member from the University of Oklahoma) were treated to a tour by Dr. Dougherty of the exposed tracks, and again new ones were discovered, including perhaps the most perfect track ever found.[5] (This recently exposed track was in a most vulnerable position, and within one year of its discovery had completely eroded away.)

At the suggestion of Dr. Harold Slusher and the author, ICR agreed to sponsor a large investigation in July, 1976, and when the time came, about 50 volunteer workers from around the country showed up to help, including Mike Turnage who was enjoying partial remission from the cancer that would take his life within a year.

Much to the chagrin of all concerned, however, a heavy rainstorm sent a "four-foot wall of water" crashing down the Paluxy on the evening before work was to begin, leaving the water level high and the water muddy throughout the ten days of work.

Not all was lost, however. Fred Beierle and Dick Caster, partially sponsored by the Bible-Science Association, had obtained from the owner permission to work on the property adjacent to the rock layer where Taylor and Turnage had done most of their work.

Fred Beierle and Dick Caster excavated the riverbank with a backhoe in an effort to intersect the previously known human trails.

By using a backhoe they excavated down to the print layer, some twenty or so feet away from the river bank. With Mike Turnage's aid he located the proper spot to dig, in hopes that he could intercept the human trail Turnage had followed in 1971. Unfortunately, no new human prints were found, but a great deal of valuable experience resulted.[6]

In fact, in the summer of 1977, Beierle was back again, not to dig this time, but to re-expose the entire rock ledge studied only a portion at a time by Taylor and Turnage. Representatives from many creationist organizations were there, including the author from ICR, who simultaneously conducted a thorough study of the geology of the area and mapped the location of all known prints. This report comprises the bulk of Chapter 10 and the Appendix of this book.

Wilbur Fields, professor at Ozark Bible College, who had visited the site in 1977, decided to lead another investigation in August of 1978 in the same location that ICR had tried to study in 1976. Prospects looked bleak when some of the worst rains in its history flooded central Texas (30 inches in 2 days). But amazingly, although within three miles other rivers were overflowing their banks, the Paluxy was bone dry. Fields, Beierle, and Dougherty were able to clean and study many sites previously inaccessible.[7]

Walter DiPietro, a Dallas scientist who had assisted the author in 1976 also returned to the Paluxy and effectively cleaned off the shelf at the Taylor site, and conditions for photography were unexcelled. The author and Tom Henderson arrived a short time later and, although no startling new human trails were found, much documentation was accomplished which will be discussed in later chapters.

Another investigation was carried out by investigators from Loma Linda University, a strongly creationist Seventh-Day Adventist school in California. In the 1960's Robert Gentry, an Adventist professor at Columbia Union College, had acquired two of the questionable tracks first seen in the 1930's. His interest was so strong that he brought earth-moving equipment to Glen Rose in the hopes of finding evidence still in the river bed. The tracks he had obtained were composed of a certain yellowish limestone with raindrop impressions in it. After attempting to follow the leads of some of the Glen Rose residents, however, he left empty-handed, unable to locate new man-like tracks or the yellowish limestone.

In 1974, several science professors from Loma Linda University traveled to Glen Rose to see footprints visible there. They saw the prints, or at least those easily exposed, and concluded that they were not made by humans, but that the elongated markings were made by three-toed dinosaurs in rather hard mud, only the central toe leaving an impression.[8]

For reasons discussed in Chapter 8, this author disagrees with the conclusions of the Loma Linda group, but the reader should be aware that these highly qualified scientists, who certainly do believe that man and dinosaur lived together, and who would welcome firm evidence, do not feel that these prints are human.

References for Chapter 4

1. Turnage, Mike (unpublished report to ICR), 1971.
2. Turnage, Mike, (unpublished report to ICR), 1972.
3. Ware, James (unpublished summary), June, 1971.
4. Dougherty, Cecil, *Valley of the Giants,* 5th Ed., Glen Rose, 1976 (published by author).
5. Morris, John D., "The Paluxy River Tracks," ICR "Impact" Series No. 35, May, 1976.
6. Beierle, Fred, *Man, Dinosaurs, and History,* Prosser, Washington: Perfect Printing, 1977.
7. Fields, Wilbur, see both *Retracing Paluxy River Tracks,* 1977, and *Paluxy River Explorations,* 1980, Joplin, MO: Ozark Bible College.
8. Neufield, Berney, "Dinosaur Tracks and Giant Men," *Origins,* V. 2, No. 2, 1975.

Chapter 5

The Geological Column versus The Biblical Account

Almost every student who has ever taken a course in geology has been required to memorize the geologic timetable, which shows the relative positions of the supposed geologic ages and the stages of evolutionary development, based on the fossil record. Specific names and dates may vary to a minor degree between charts, but all show a gradual evolution of life from the late Precambrian period up to the present. The fossil record is sparse and highly speculative prior to the Cambrian, which is thought to have witnessed the beginning of abundant marine invertebrate and early vertebrate life. The Paleozoic Era, thought to have lasted from about 600 million years ago to about 225 million years ago, was dominated by marine animals and primitive plants, with few land animals. The Mesozoic Era, from 225-70 million years ago, is known as the age of the reptiles, and dinosaurs are thought to have ruled the earth at this time. With the extinction

THE GEOLOGIC COLUMN

Eras	Characteristics According to the Evolution Model	AGES IN MILLIONS OF YEARS BEFORE PRESENT	Characteristic Life	Characteristics According to the Creation Model
PALEOZOIC	Rise of modern plants and animals, including man. Ice Age.	0 2	QUATERNARY	Post-flood development of modern world by modern processes. --- Ice Age. Effects of post-flood glaciation and pluviation. Less volcanism and tectonism. --- Final stages of flood and early post-flood activity. Water drains into larger basins. Erosion of previously deposited material. Domination of poorly consolidated continental sediments and fossils.
	Rise of mammals and development of highest plants.	65	TERTIARY	
MESOZOIC	Modernized angiosperms, foraminifers, insects abundant. Extinction of dinosaurs.	135	CRETACEOUS	Intermediate stages of flood, with mixtures of marine and continental deposits. Land completely covered. Extinction of all land creatures, including dinosaurs. Oceans begin to deepen or widen at end of this phase.
	First reptilian birds, primitive angiosperms, highest insects, etc.	190	JURASSIC	
	Earliest dinosaurs, flying reptiles, marine reptiles, and primitive mammals. Cycads and conifers and modern corals common. Earliest ammonites.	225	TRIASSIC	
	Rise of primitive reptiles. Earliest cycads, conifers, and modern corals. Extinction of trilobites.		PERMIAN	Waters nearing maximum height. Pri-

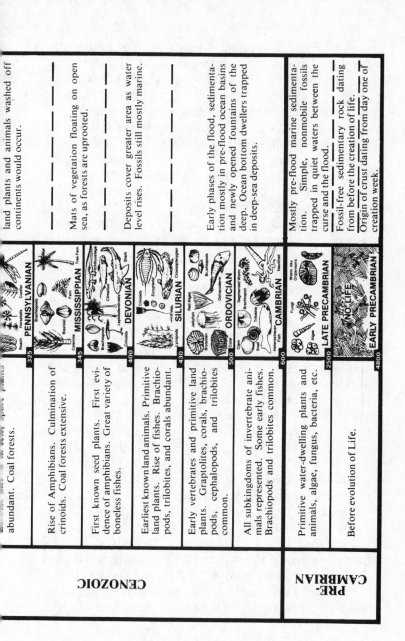

land plants and animals washed off continents would occur.

Mats of vegetation floating on open sea, as forests are uprooted.

Deposits cover greater area as water level rises. Fossils still mostly marine.

Early phases of the flood, sedimentation mostly in pre-flood ocean basins and newly opened fountains of the deep. Ocean bottom dwellers trapped in deep-sea deposits.

Mostly pre-flood marine sedimentation. Simple, nonmobile fossils trapped in quiet waters between the curse and the flood.

Fossil-free sedimentary rock dating from before the creation of life.

Origin of crust dating from day one of creation week.

PENNSYLVANIAN — 325
MISSISSIPPIAN — 345
DEVONIAN — 400
SILURIAN — 430
ORDOVICIAN — 500
CAMBRIAN — 600
LATE PRECAMBRIAN — 2500
EARLY PRECAMBRIAN — 4800

abundant. Coal forests.

Rise of Amphibians. Culmination of crinoids. Coal forests extensive.

First known seed plants. First evidence of amphibians. Great variety of boneless fishes.

Earliest known land animals. Primitive land plants. Rise of fishes. Brachiopods, trilobites, and corals abundant.

Early vertebrates and primitive land plants. Graptolites, corals, brachiopods, cephalopods, and trilobites common.

All subkingdoms of invertebrate animals represented. Some early fishes. Brachiopods and trilobites common.

Primitive water-dwelling plants and animals, algae, fungus, bacteria, etc.

Before evolution of Life.

CENOZOIC

PRE-CAMBRIAN

of the dinosaurs, land mammals and birds supposedly developed during the time known as the Cenozoic Era, and finally about 7-10 million years ago the ancestors of man appeared. The direct ancestors of modern man, walking upright, developed only within the last few million years, according to some recent claims.

Creationists have long objected to the use of this "geological column" which has never been found in its complete form in any one location around the world, pointing out serious scientific and philosophical errors associated with it. Darwin was aware of some of these problems in his day, but in his writings maintained a belief that eventually these problems would be solved.

One tremendous problem is the presence of regular systematic gaps in the fossil record. For instance, there are cats in the fossil record and dogs in the fossil record, but nothing in between. There is no evidence that one ever evolved into the other or that both came from a common ancestor, indicating that as long as cats and dogs have existed they have been either cats or dogs—nothing in between. This problem is magnified many times when the huge gaps between major kinds of animals are considered. As far as the actual fossil data are concerned, there is no real objective evidence of the evolution of one basic kind of organism into another.[1]

Another problem for the evolutionists is the fact that most, if not all, formations imply rapid erosion, transportation and deposition of sediments, not a gradual accumulation. Indeed, fossils of any kind require rapid burial in sediments that must quickly turn to stone, or the organism will disintegrate (or be devoured by scavengers) without having an opportunity to become fossilized. A fish, for example, will never sink to the bottom of the ocean and remain intact until it is slowly buried and lithified. If it was not trapped and buried quickly, it would just decompose in the common manner. Other geologic features—grading, folding, erosion patterns, etc.—all seem to show that these events happened quickly, not over long periods of time.

The problem of time is confounded when animal tracks are considered. How long does a footprint in mud last before it is eroded or altered? An hour? A day? Until the next rain? Certainly it does not last for millions of years while the mud is gradually turning to stone. It must happen quickly. The prints must be preserved rapidly or they will be destroyed.[2]

Consider the case at the Paluxy. Both dinosaur and man-like tracks are preserved with excellent detail, side by side, in the same rock layer. According to the evolutionary time scale, dinosaurs died out about 70 million years ago, and man appeared only in the last few million years.

Thus, evolutionists face a dilemma. There is, in their perspective, a 65-million-year gap between the extinction of the dinosaur and the advent of man, a gap during which there should have been no dinosaurs and no men. But in the limestone layers in the Paluxy River, the fossil tracks seem to indicate that man and dinosaurs lived not only at the same place, but at the same time! To make matters worse, the particular formation in which the prints are found is known as the Glen Rose Limestone, designated early Cretaceous, which supposedly was laid down early in the Cretaceous period and thought to be 120 million years old. The Trinity Group, of which the Glen Rose Limestone is a part, has been judged to be the oldest Cretaceous layer in Central Texas.

In the April, 1974, issue of *National Geographic,* Mary Leaky reported the discovery of human footprints in strata dated at least 3.6 million years old (by uniformitarian methods) in East Africa. The thought of humans walking erect so long ago caused a minor revision of the concepts of the origin and evolution of man, but not to the degree that the Paluxy River evidence would do. Pictures of the Leakey footprints were sufficiently human to convince most of the scientific community, but a comparison of those prints with the Paluxy prints shows that the prints in Glen Rose are much better, certainly retaining more of the diagnostic features of the foot.

And yet the Paluxy evidence is not accepted. Since it cannot be made to fit into the evolutionary scheme without a major revision, most evolutionists prefer either to ignore the evidence, to ascribe it to an un-

The best footprint found by Mary Leakey in East Africa, which has convinced most of its human source, does not compare favorably with many of the prints found in the Paluxy. Photo by Peter Jones.
© *National Geographic.*

Specimen of carbonized wood found at the Taylor site was dated at 38,000 years old.

known animal, or to ridicule the credentials of the discoverers. Some uniformitarian scientists, convinced of the genuineness of the Paluxy data, have contended that the coexistence of man and dinosaur does not disprove evolution, but does suggest a revision of the geologic timetable.

But what a revision! Since evolutionists estimate about 600 million years for the evolution of all life, from the single cell to man, this revision would wipe out at least 20% of the history of life. It does not matter whether man existed 120 million years ago, or whether dinosaurs survived until recently. In either case the geologic column is vastly in error in the most recent section. And if we cannot trust it in the most recent geologic ages, which should be the least altered and least subjective, how can we possibly trust it in the more remote past?

Several samples of plant remains found in these strata provide the only real physical data for establishing a firm date according to uniformitarian assumptions. They were dated by the carbon-14 dating method and the results are interesting, even if not very informative. The carbon-14 dating technique has been shown in recent years to have some very questionable assumptions, and many believe that the older carbon-14 dates are higher than they should be. One of these faulty assumptions has to do with the global rates of production and decay of carbon-14, long thought to be equal, but now known to be quite different. An adjusted equation may still leave much to be desired, but it is thought by most geologists that carbon-14 dates are at least reasonably accurate, especially within the past few thousand years.

The first two specimens (found at the Taylor Site), were sent to a dating lab by Taylor with no explanation as to their origin. One was dated at approximately 38,000 B.P. ("before present" dated from 1950) and the other at 39,000 B.P.[3] These two large dates are somewhat meaningless since they are near the limit of the method's range. A later specimen (found at the McFall ledge), was dated at the same laboratory at about 890 B.P.,[4] which yields an actual date of 1060 A.D.! The most recent effort dated a carbonized branch found downstream near the second crossing at 12,800 years B.P.,[5] even though it and all the other specimens were found in rock thought to be 120 million years old.

It is not suggested here that any of these dates are correct. If the layer dates from the Flood of Noah, as creationists allege, then all the dates are significantly in error. What is suggested here is that the carbon-14 dating method, which so frequently gives scattered results for material of similar "age" is very questionable, and should not be trusted until these problems can be solved.

A well-preserved piece of woody material found at the ledge near the Mc-Fall site. It was dated as only 890 years old, even though the layer in which it was found has been dated at 120,000,000 years.

Carbonized stick found imbedded in the Glen Rose Limestone by Beierle, Fields, and others. It was dated by the UCLA laboratory as 12,800 years old.

The fact is, regardless of the age of the strata, man and dinosaur did exist at the same place and time, if the "man-tracks" are genuinely human. And the question is, "What would this discrepancy in the geologic timetable do to the theory of organic evolution, thought to have occurred over vast spans of geologic time?"

Evolutionists have long asserted that the main evidence for evolution can be found in the fossil record. Evolutionary time periods have been identified by the use of index fossils, organisms represented now by their fossils which are thought to have existed only during a certain span of time in the past. But if man (walking upright with modern feet, therefore modern man) lived 120 million years ago, then certainly all of the supposed pre-men or missing links should be interpreted as descendants, not ancestors, of modern man. And there remains no hint whatsoever of the ancestors of man in pre-Cretaceous time.

Man, of course, is one of the index fossils of recent strata, just as dinosaurs are in Mesozoic strata. The demonstration that these index fossils are unreliable (and certainly, these are thought to be among the most reliable index fossils) would deal a serious blow to the evolutionary time scale.

Creationists, however, do not face such a dilemma. This evidence fits quite well not only with the over-all creation model of a young earth and nonuniform processes governing much of the past, but also with a great deal of other data indicating that all of the earth's inhabitants lived at essentially the same time.

The Biblical account itself speaks of dinosaurs, as would be expected if it reflects an accurate history of the earth. On the fifth day of creation week, as recorded in Gen. 1:21, great "whales" or "sea monsters" (depending on the translation) were created.

Actually neither translation is accurate. The Hebrew word is "tannin" and is in most places properly translated as "dragons." Dragon legends are part of the folklore of nearly every culture around the world and were generally regarded as huge fearsome beasts. But myths usually have a kernel of truth behind them, obscured by the telling and retelling, and since so many remotely related cultures have similar myths, it implies that all cultures either have a common origin or that all of them encountered "dragons" of some sort (or both).[6]

Detailed descriptions of dragons are provided in the Biblical Book of Job, chapters 40 and 41. The "behemoth" in 40:15 is described as an animal with a huge midsection, a tail like a cedar tree, bones as strong as iron, living in swampy regions, and as one of the largest creatures that God ever made. The description seems to fit what modern science has surmised about brontosaur-type dinosaurs more than anything else. The "leviathan" in chapter 41, was an extremely fierce sea monster that apparently spent time both in the sea and on land. He had huge teeth and scales, although he was evidently air-breathing, as reptiles are. In verses 18-22 the Bible claims that he could actually breathe fire! (Perhaps this provides insight into the common tradition of fire-breathing dragons.) He was absolutely without fear and was proclaimed "king" over all other large, proud animals. Fossil remains of certain dinosaurs fit this description.

So the discovery of human and dinosaur tracks together should not surprise the Bible-believing Christian. Such discoveries would be necessarily rare, but a year-long, mountain-covering, geologically-significant worldwide flood, could certainly generate conditions which could occasionally have come together to preserve such prints.

Since the Bible indicates that dinosaurs lived before the Flood of Noah, and likewise had contact with men after the Flood, as in the case of Job, it stands to reason that some of them may have survived the watery catastrophe. Perhaps those who were more agile in the water were able to swim through the turmoil, at least in representative numbers, but that does not solve the problem of the land dinosaurs. It may be that Noah took members of the land kinds on board the Ark, as God had decreed that two of each kind of land-dwelling, air-breathing creatures were to be placed on the Ark. He did not have to take adult animals, and indeed probably would have taken younger, more virile, and therefore smaller, individuals on board, those more likely to reproduce when the Flood was over. It is also possible that he took dinosaur eggs on the Ark, eliminating the need for so much food and space.

References for Chapter 5

1. Gish, Duane T., *Evolution: The Fossils Say No!* San Diego: CLP Publishers, 1979.
2. Morris, Henry M., *Scientific Creationism,* San Diego: CLP Publishers, 1974.
3. Dated by Isotopes, Westwood Laboratory, Sample Nos. I-4526 and I-4527, Nov. 21, 1969.
4. Dated by Teledyne Isotopes, Westwood Laboratory, Sample No. I-6477, May 17, 1972.
5. Dated by UCLA, Sample No. UCLA 2088, Oct. 23, 1978.
6. Gish, Duane T., *Dinosaurs: Those Terrible Lizards,* San Diego: CLP Publishers, 1977, pp. 50-60.

Chapter 6

Geologic Setting

No discussion of the Paluxy River tracks could be complete without placing them in the proper geological and stratigraphic setting. Most of the opposition to the implications of the discovery comes from those in geologic fields, and this chapter will attempt to answer those questions before they are asked.

Throughout the area in question the Paluxy River bottom consists primarily of a hard layer of limestone, in most places rather resistant to erosion. Although several layers are known to have prints in them, this one layer contains the most distinct prints and other surface features which make it unique. This bed has no specific name, but the overall stratigraphy has been worked out.

The oldest (lowest) Cretaceous rocks in Central Texas belong to the Trinity Group, which has, in turn, been divided into three major formations, the Twin Mountains, Glen Rose, and Paluxy Formations. Lowermost is the Twin Mountains Formation, a mixed terrigenous clastic sequence,[1] and "composed of fine to medium-grained, subrounded, medium-sorted, highly compacted but friable sandstone."[2] It is quite easily eroded, but no erosional period existed between the deposition of the Twin Mountains and the Glen Rose Limestone, which conformably overlies it and comprises the second formation in the Trinity Group. It is the Glen Rose Limestone which contains both the dinosaur and man-like tracks.

According to the *Geologic Atlas of Texas,* the Glen Rose Formation is:

Limestone, alternating with units composed of variable amounts of clay, marl, and sand. Limestone, distinctly bedded, in part with variable amounts of clay, silt, and sand, soft to hard, in various shades of brownish yellow and gray. Thickness 40-200 feet, thins northward.[3]

Nagle further explains that the formation:

LOCAL GEOLOGIC SECTION

CRETACEOUS	BASAL CRETACEOUS (TRINITY GROUP)	PALUXY FORMATION (SANDSTONE)

GLEN ROSE FORMATION (LIMESTONE)

UPPER GLEN ROSE (MANY LAYERS)

THORP SPRING MEMBER

LOWER GLEN ROSE (MANY LAYERS)

MARKER BED 6"-12"
CLAY OR FOSSIL LAYER 14"
MAIN PRINT LAYER 24"

PALUXY RIVER

PRINTS

TWIN MOUNTAINS FORMATION (ARENACEOUS, PRIMARILY SANDSTONE)

6-A

The local geologic section showing the three formations in the Trinity Group. The bottom layer of the lowermost member of the Glen Rose Limestone comprises the river bottom in the study area and contains nearly all of the well preserved prints.

Consists of alternating beds of resistant and weak rocks that form distinctive stairstep topography, the resistant beds are either pure limestone, usually a spar-cemented calcarenite, or carbonate-cemented sandstone, whereas the weak beds are dolomite, dolomitic limestone, shaley limestone, mudstone, or uncemented sand.[4]

Both the Glen Rose Limestone and the overlying Paluxy Sandstone are relatively flat lying, but some amount of erosion is thought to have occurred before the Paluxy formation was deposited, or during its deposition. This unconformity is suggested by local

Mike Turnage and Debbie Bainer investigating potential footprint site. Note large blocks of grey Thorp Spring member remnants.

truncation of some of the upper beds of the Glen Rose.[5] Others feel that the truncations only represent local drainage and refer to the two beds as conformable, with no erosional sequence involved.[6-7]

Davis describes this overlying Paluxy Sandstone as:
Homogeneous, fine-grained, compact, white to reddish-brown quartz sand with scattered lenses and laminae of dark, impure clay.[8]

All three of the Trinity Formations, the Twin Mountains, the Glen Rose Limestone, and the Paluxy Sandstone are present in outcrop in Somervell County, each making up about one-third of the sequence. However, each of these formations divide into members, and each member may contain numerous individual beds.

In the study area the Glen Rose Limestone contains three members. The upper and lower members consist of numerous carbonate beds alternating with terrigenous clastic beds. The middle member consists of only one bed, the Thorp Spring Member. Our interest centers in the lowest member, containing in places up to twenty beds, and although tracks have been seen in several layers, the layer containing the best and most dinosaur tracks is the lowest bed in the member.

To some, the succession of beds in the lower Glen Rose Limestone suggests a cycle involved in its deposition, but the suggestion is only tentative since there is no typical cycle. The beds themselves tend to be limited in extent, and over a matter of miles the sequence will vary widely. Of the seven or so cycles encountered the members all seem to be associated with rather shallow water deposition, but authorities disagree as to the specific mechanism. Nagle concludes:
Facies succession indicates that each cycle represents a subtidal to supratidal [below and above mean sea level] respectively, [but still

within the tidal variation] depositional regime'
transit; cycles are regressional, with the trans-
gressional phase being poorly developed if at
all.[9]

In other words, during each cycle, although sea level
rose and sank with respect to the land, most if not all
of the deposits were laid down during the time when
the sea was retreating or lowering.

Conversely, Davis claims that the "Strata of
the Trinity Group were deposited on the broad
relatively flat central Texas platform over
which epicontinental seas slowly transgressed
from the south and east . . . . The gentle sea-
ward slope and low relief of the surface on
which the Glen Rose Formation was deposited
produced an extremely broad tidal zone with
extensive facies tracts roughly paralleling the
shoreline . . . .

"With continued transgression, the Glen
Rose shoreline progressed farther to the north-
west. Low to moderate rates of marine sedimentation coupled with periodic influx of terrigenous material allowed deposition to keep
pace with the slowly rising sea level."[10]

While Davis and Nagle agree that the sediments
which made up the Trinity Group were all deposited in
shallow water, Davis feels that a regional rise of sea
level with respect to the land is responsible, while
Nagle postulates a cycle of rising and falling, with few
deposits representing the rising phase. Both cannot be
right, but geologic evidence is sketchy and subjective.

The Glen Rose Limestone is not an insignificant
bed. Outcrops of it can be seen all over Texas with the
possible exception of the Panhandle area, but even in
these areas some remnants of the Trinity Group have
been found. Its major band of outcrop extends south-

erly from the north central area of Texas, around the east and south of the Llano Uplift. It varies from 10 feet thick near the Oklahoma border to about 750 feet thick in central Texas and is reported to be several thousand feet thick in northern Mexico. Dinosaur tracks and markings are found in over twenty locations throughout the state in various layers of the Glen Rose. The characteristics of the formation are broadly similar throughout, and it is thought that the depositional mechanism, the source area, etc., are essentially the same in all areas.

Even though there is some disagreement as to the geologic history of the formation, all agree that the Glen Rose was laid down in shallow water, either within or just above or below tidal and wave action. Physical indications which point to this are worm burrows in the surfaces of the beds, poorly developed channel or drainage structures, low angle cross-bedding, layers of poorly sorted shell fragments, fossils found in the living positions, ripple marks, rain drop marks, and animal tracks. The uniformitarian model of deposition, of course, concludes that the deposits formed slowly, over several million years, by accumulation of particles and organisms in the near-shore zone of shallowest water and low energy caused by shoaling in the nearby basinward zone as the sea either transgressed or oscillated many times.

But shallow water deposition is a relatively high-energy deposition and these indicators can also be interpreted as evidence for rapid deposition. It will be shown in Chapter 7 that these beds must have been deposited quickly, one right after the other, with no time break in between. Otherwise, features such as animal tracks would have been obliterated, and organisms would not have been buried alive in their living positions to be fossilized later.

References for Chapter 6

1. Fisher, W.L., and Rodda, P.U., "Lower Cretaceous Sands of Texas: Stratigraphy and Resources," *Bureau of Economic Geology Reprint of Investigations,* No. 59, p. 3.
2. Davis, Keith W., "Stratigraphy and Depositional Environments of the Glen Rose Formation, North-Central Texas," *Baylor Geologic Society Bulletin,* No. 26, 1974, p. 10.
3. *The Geologic Atlas of Texas, Dallas Sheet* (University of Texas at Austin), 1972.
4. Nagle, J. Steward, "Glen Rose Cycles and Facies, Paluxy River Valley, Somervell County, Texas," *Bureau of Economic Geology Circular,* No. 68-1, 1968, p. 2.
5. Amsbury, D.L., "Caliche Soil Profiles in Lower Cretaceous Rocks in Central Texas," presented at Geological Society of America meeting in New Orleans, 1967, p. 4.
6. Nagle, p. 5.
7. *Geological Atlas of Texas.*
8. Davis, p. 9.
9. Nagle, p. 1.
10. Davis, pp. 24, 25.

Chapter 7

Formation of the Tracks

Attempts to understand the phenomena of erosion, transportation, and deposition of sediments is not a new one. Hydraulic engineers have been researching the question for fifty years or so. Their need to know is an immediate and practical one, because they are responsible for the safety and stability of water-related structures, (e.g., silting of canals, reservoirs, and harbors; land erosion, bank stability; river meandering). The laboratory empirical and analytical studies have answered many of the questions about the potential of moving water, but the phenomena are extremely complex and much work remains to be done.

Geologists share an interest in sedimentation processes when an attempt is made to reconstruct the geologic history of a formation. In doing so, they rely on their familiarity with present geologic events and processes and extrapolate them back into the past. It is thought that the degree of reliability of their conclusions varies directly with their knowledge of the present. But the geologist's approach to sedimentation has, with few exceptions, been qualitative and descriptive, as opposed to quantitative and mathematical, even though the engineering experiments and observations in the present represent the "state-of-the-art" in hydraulic processes. If, with the use of empirical and analytical equations, hydrologists are hesitant to place too much confidence in predictions of what will happen in the near future, then it seems that careful geologists would be reluctant to make statements about conditions in the remote past, especially when made without the aid of modern studies.

Consider the interpretation of a near-shore environment for the Glen Rose Limestone, which contains thousands of animal tracks. Investigating geologists see the evidence of low angle cross-bedding, ripple marks, tracks, etc., and conclude that a lagoon, bay, or tidal flat must have existed for a long time period and the sediment layers were deposited in this environment. Unfortunately, what is known about hydraulic sedimentation and erosion seems to preclude this ex-

Bank of the Paluxy River showing layering of numerous beds, indicating individual deposition conditions lasted only a short time.

Photo by Dougherty.

planation and, since there is another model of depositional history which seems to fit both the geological and
the theoretical data much better, the long-age interpretation for this formation is not necessary.

Notice Roland Bird's conclusion about the preservation of the dinosaur tracks:

> When animal tracks were preserved in pre-
> historic times, the process was a simple one.
> Here, dinosaurs—in this case large carnivores
> —had crossed the muds of shoreline flats in
> quest of prey; later, gentle water currents cov-
> ered the still distinct tracks with layers of set-
> tling silt and marine deposits. Layers con-
> tinued to accumulate upon the subsiding sur-
> face. In the course of millions of years the
> whole eventually solidified into stone. Erosion
> and elevation of the land laid the tracks bare
> again as impressions in hardened rock.

Certainly it should not be questioned that erosion
has once again exposed the tracks, but Bird's interpretation of the deposition process is too simple.
Much more enters into the deposition and hardening
of sediments that he did not take into account. To
begin with, tracks of animals made on a wet sandy
beach will probably be gone within a matter of hours,
certainly by the next high tide. If the ground is of a
more silty or clayey nature, the same process which
saturated it to begin with is capable of wiping it clean
once again, just as it supposedly did before the episode
started. Any water action that conceivably could cover the prints with a layer of protecting sediments
would wipe out the prints in the process. Even wind
and rain will see to it that the prints would shortly
disappear, just as they are now doing to the prints in
the Paluxy River bottom, even though these latter are
in hard stone.

Layering here shows a resistant limestone bed overlain by a conglomerate layer and underlain by a fine clay layer.

The original prints must have been made in a recently deposited layer of mud which happened to have a chemical cementing agent present in it at the time of deposition. Such an extensive layer of sediments would imply a great amount of water covering the area and depositing its load as its energy decreased. Next, the water either drained off completely or nearly so in order for animals of various sizes to make their prints in the already hardening sediments. The prints were temporarily frozen in place, but as we have seen, they do not last but a few years in crystalline limestone and would be eroded within a short time indeed in any somewhat plastic material. The only way that some would be preserved with any of the features distinct at all would be for the newly deposited layer to harden sufficiently within a few hours to withstand the next onslaught of inundation and deposition of an overlying layer. In the case of the Glen Rose prints, all of the prints are either in a thick claystone or in limestone covered by a banded claystone. Clay is usually quite impervious to water flow and would have provided protection against water action for the prints as the host rock finished its transformation into stone. The clay layer above the man print layer is filled with literally millions of fossil clams, which can easily be pulled from outcrops. Clams which die a natural death would open up, separate, and be broken. Many of these clams, however, are whole and tightly shut as a living clam would be if it were in danger. Evidently, these clams were buried alive in the thick deposit of clay, which also served to protect the newly formed animal tracks.

That it took neither one of these layers long to be deposited is obvious from the nature of both layers and their fossils. That there was no significant time-break between deposition of the layers is obvious be-

Museum specimens of fossils found in the Glen Rose Limestone. Note: Portions of the original shell of the clam have been preserved.

In the fossil layer are literally billions of fossil clams tightly closed, indicating rapid burial while still alive.

cause the prints were not eroded away. Within the
Paluxy River area, prints are found in several of the
individual beds and so the logic can be extended to include the entire lower member of the Glen Rose Formation and eventually to include all formations within the Trinity Group.

As a matter of fact, a large portion of the geologic
column can be interpreted as having been deposited
rapidly, as part of a single great catastrophe. Each
bed could have been laid down quickly, and if there is
no evidence of significant erosion, then there could
have been no time gap between. There are erosional
surfaces (unconformities) in the column, but there is

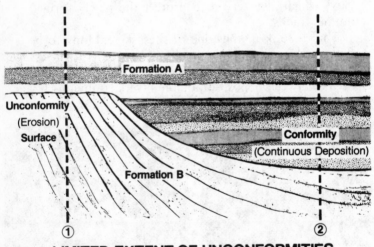

LIMITED EXTENT OF UNCONFORMITIES

7-E

*The fact that there are no worldwide unconformities indicates that there
were no major gaps between the deposition of successive formations.
Since the formations were formed rapidly, the entire geologic column
could have been laid down by a single event.*

no such thing as a worldwide unconformity, most of them being rather local in extent. Even in cases of large unconformities, if they are traced laterally far enough they are seen to disappear, and the beds again indicate that in that location no erosional time break took place. Every bed of sufficient lateral extent, somewhere grades conformably into the next higher bed.

It is reasonable to assume that the amount and type of sediment that can be transported by moving water is a function of flow-depth and velocity, the channel slope, the density, specific weight, and viscosity of the fluid and the size of sediment grain. It may also be a function of the temperature, channel roughness, chemical content of the water, state of flow, and perhaps other unknown factors. Numerous empirical formulas have been derived to approximate the carrying potential of the stream. Typical of these formulas is the following, developed from data published by Albertson and Garde at Colorado State University:

$$G_S = \frac{1.36 \ W \ V^4 \ n^3}{k^3 \ d^{1.5} \ D \ (10^{15})}$$

where G_S represents the total number of pounds of sediment being transported each second past any given point in the stream; W is stream width in feet; V is velocity of flow in feet per second; n is a roughness coefficient; depth of flow D and particle diameter d are in feet; k is the kinetic viscosity of the water, which reflects the effect of temperature.[2]

This equation and other similar ones are known to give workable results, although its predictions are only approximate. It measures the amount of sediment a stream of known dimensions can carry for a given set of conditions. Any available sediment above this value will not be transported, but will remain at rest or be deposited. A change in any one of these factors will alter the character of the deposits.

Each sedimentary stratum represents a constant set of all the various factors which control the sedimentation process. Since such uniform conditions can persist for only a very brief time, each stratum represents only a few minutes of sedimentation. All of the strata in a given formation are normally parallel and continuous, thus representing uninterrupted deposition. Even when an unconformity is encountered—at the top of a formation, for example, such an unconformity is always of only limited extent, and the deposition process is continuous beyond its limits.

In this way almost the whole geologic column can be accounted for in terms of one hydraulic event, worldwide in scope and capable of eroding, transporting and depositing great amounts of sediment. This, of course, could be the great Flood mentioned in the Bible, a tremendous cataclysm which would have totally restructured the surface of the globe.

This admittedly incomplete discussion of hydraulic sedimentation has been included to show that any reasonable conclusions regarding past geologic events must take into account many factors. Simplistic answers based only on superficial and qualitative knowledge of present sedimentologic and topographic features are unlikely to be correct. Bird's conclusion, quoted earlier in this chapter, appears to fall into this category.

References for Chapter 7

1. Bird, Roland T., "We Captured a Live Brontosaur," *National Geographic,* May, 1954, pp. 711-712.
2. Morris, Henry M. and Wiggert, James M., *Applied Hydraulics in Engineering,* New York: John Wiley and Sons, Publ., 1972, pp. 465-467.

Chapter 8

Proper Identification of the Tracks

Seldom does one find a perfect track of any sort of animal in the Glen Rose Formation, one that shows all the features of the paw or foot. This is to be expected, of course, for an animal walking in mud or wet sand without consciously trying to leave good tracks will slip, change stride, alter direction, stop, or do other things that might mar his footprints.

This is especially true in the case of human tracks, as one can easily prove for himself. (Walk along a beach, mud flat, or fresh snow and notice the variation in track detail, size, direction, and stride length.) It would be nice to discover perfect human footprints that showed all the features of the human foot, but those that are found are more realistic, seemingly just what one would expect.

The lack of precise detail on the prints has prompted some evolutionists to claim that the man-like prints are erosional features caused by moving water, not tracks at all. To be sure, nature can produce some amazing simulations at times and proper identification is not always easy. Several criteria have been established to help make the determination, and at least some, if not all, of these should be present if a marking is to be identified either as a human track or a track of some kind of animal, as opposed to merely an erosional or deformational feature.

Two of the most important of these criteria have been used by the local Glen Rose enthusiasts for decades and both are consistent with logic. Walking in mud not only produces an indentation where the foot sank down, but invariably also produces a "mud up-push," a place where the surrounding mud has been pushed up higher than it was before. Generally this occurs around the outside of the foot in those areas where most of the weight is borne. In the dinosaur prints, the largest up-pushes usually are found around

This marking is obviously a track of some kind. Note how the material adjacent to the print has been pushed up higher than it was before. An erosional feature would not produce such a "mud up-push." Films for Christ. Photo by Taylor.

A human-like footprint found in New Mexico. Note distinctive "mud up-push" at heel and elsewhere and the diagnostic "pressure striations" parallel to the contour of the print (situated on a steep slope, allowing some insight into mud deformations below print).

the toe area, but for the man prints, the location is more varied, evidently representing a more varied stride. They are found primarily behind the heel and adjacent to the big toe and the ball of the foot. "Erosional processes" would not leave a "mud up-push" or pressure ridges around an elongated erosional marking, features which are common in the Paluxy River.

Another telltale feature which has been known to the Glen Rose residents and scientists alike is not so easy to discern, but again, it is consistent with simple logic. The weight of the man or animal making the track not only deforms the mud, but causes vertical displacement below the foot. As the foot forces the mud down into the subsurface, the mud is compacted, with the amount of compaction decreasing with depth. If the mud has any layers of discoloration, variations in texture, or changes in composition, these laminations will deform beneath the impression.

Only in special circumstances can these pressure striations be seen in the field, since obviously they are beneath the surface. But if the rock layer happens to be broken off near the print or if the print was made on a steep slope, then they are visible. Those who made their living removing and selling the prints during the depression of the 1930's would sometimes chip off a small section, just to demonstrate the authenticity of the print. Some of the prints which had been removed were taken to scientific laboratories and sawn open, and even though some proved to be mere carvings, some did contain the telltale laminations.

In some cases even this test is not infallible. If the original mud were completely homogeneous, with no bands present, deformation lines may not be present after the print was made. There may be lines of metamorphosis or change in crystallization below the track, only visible with a magnifying glass. Mottled "incipient metamorphism" also might be present. In some cases, evidently when the mud flowed readily, the material would have been simply displaced into an "uppush" without leaving any lines of stratification. This was shown several years ago by Dr. George Westcott, who made footprints in wet homogeneous plaster to study the problem. The absence of the deformed laminations does not, therefore, *disprove* genuineness, but the special circumstances necessary to prohibit formation of the lines would be rare.

Conversely, the presence of laminations which are not deformed, but are traceable to the edge of the print where they end abruptly, *are* sufficient to show that the "print" is not a true print, but a natural feature or a carving.

At the present time it is illegal to remove any track

from its original position, thus limiting this method of analysis. Those that have been sawn open, in which the depressed laminations or distinctive metamorphic features were visible, have included dinosaur, human, and a large cat-like print. There is no conceivable way for such markings to have been formed by erosion or subsurface water flow, not when they are parallel or related to the bottom contour of the foot.

Frequently in the Paluxy a dinosaur footprint is found by itself, without being part of a trail, and since a dinosaur track is usually quite distinctive and quite deep, there is no trouble in determining its origin. For the most part, however, the distinction between animal tracks and erosional features must be based on the existence of a trail of tracks, in a right-left-right-left sequence, all conformable to one another in size and shape. They should be separated by a relatively con-

The downstream portion of the Taylor trail. There are over 20 footprints in left-right sequence, consistent stride and straddle, several showing good impressions. Crossing the trail, in the same rock, are two dinosaur trails. Tracks are greased.

sistent length, representing the stride of the individual
and laterally by a few inches representing the natural
straddle between the two feet. The trail should trend
in one direction; each individual track should also be
oriented in the same direction. The size of the tracks
should be reasonable when compared to its length of
stride. If a consistent trail can be followed, an erosional origin can be ruled out altogether, and there are
numerous dinosaur trails and man-like trails that fit
these criteria.

To distinguish between an animal trail and a barefoot man trail requires additional evidence. A human
trail should not only satisfy the requirements given for
any trail, but it should be that of a bipedal upright
individual. Furthermore, the prints themselves, or at
least representative prints within the trail, should have
the general features of a human foot. The ball of the
foot and the heel are generally the best preserved, since
it is on these two areas that most of the weight is con
centrated. The arch is characteristically raised and the
sloping toe line is usually visible. Individual toe depressions are rare, as would be expected, but toe markings made as the foot left the newly formed print are
frequently preserved.

Commonly, the ball of the foot leaves the deepest
impression, due to the fact that the entire weight of the
body is concentrated in this spot while walking, just
before the opposite foot strikes the ground. At this
point the heel is off the ground and mud is squeezed
up between the toes as they are pressed into the mud.
Generally, these toe ridges are too fragile to be preserved, although in some cases the one between the big
and second toes can be seen.

However, assuming that these tracks were formed at
the time of the great Flood, there is no reason to assume that all pre-Flood people walked barefoot. Ac-

cording to the Bible, civilization was at an advanced level then, and certainly some, if not all, wore shoes. During the initial stages of the Flood, many may have lost their foot coverings, but some would have salvaged them or hastily made others. Numerous tracks in the Paluxy fit the expected shape of a wrapped or covered human foot. These, of course, do not show individual toe marks, etc., and identification is more difficult. When found in sequence, with consistent straddle, stride, and dimensions present, some degree of satisfaction as to their origin can be obtained.

Other explanations have been offered seeking to credit these man-like prints to some other animal. Roland Bird, in a letter to Mike Turnage dated February 21, 1969, claimed:

> They are definitely, repeat, definitely NOT human. I am well familiar with all the fossil footprints found in the Glen Rose (Cretaceous) of Central Texas, and have seen those purported to be "human" by farmers lacking any geologic training.

> They were made by carnivorous dinosaurs wading through deep mud. When the foot was withdrawn the sides of the resulting cavity flowed inward leaving an oblong opening only faintly suggestive of the footprint of a man in the eye of the beholder. When one followed such a trail, tracks of the dinosaur were invariably found that showed all the details of a three-toed dinosaur.

> Anything else "human" exhibited or reported "found" in the area is the product of a very clever prankster with hammer and chisel.

Bird was only partially right. There are several trails of "three-toed" dinosaur tracks in which the mud has squeezed back in to cover the outer two toes, leaving

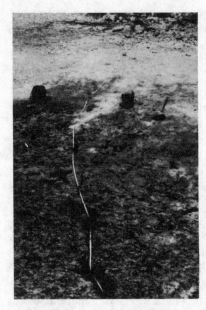

At the "Shakey Springs" section of the Paluxy River are several trails which at first glance resemble human trails (left). A close look, however, reveals three slender markings at the top of each print, remnants of dinosaur "toes."

Unidentified dinosaur track (below), showing three protrusions. These elongated prints could under some circumstances be mistaken for human prints.

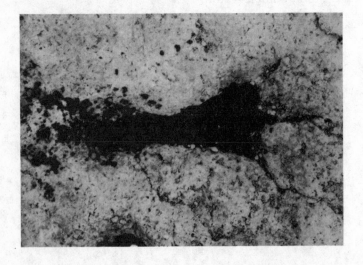

an elongated marking. Some of the reported man trails are of this kind and will be discussed in a later chapter. But there are others which are definitely not forgeries and which do not in any of their tracks show evidence of having been made by anything other than a man. Most of the best trails that are still in the river have been exposed since Bird did his work in the Paluxy and, as such, were not studied by him. Thus, his statement could not be considered all-inclusive, just as it should not be considered correct even for those exposed at that time.

One more question remains. In his sketch of the slab (shown in Chapter 2) removed for the American Museum and several universities, Bird refers to and sketches an elongated track that was moved to New York. The only explanation that he provides in the legend is "Single Giant Track." Perhaps the report of the removal of other "giant tracks" as reported earlier is not so far-fetched.

Loma Linda University scientists have recently come to a conclusion similar to the one Bird described in his letter to Turnage. While studying the prints at the Taylor site they made the following assessment:

> The tracks are one-half to one inch deep, and their general form can be described as moccasin prints. Casts were made of the entire series. Comparison of these to the Series 1 [McFall trail] elongated tracks, has led to the conclusion that at least two members of the series are badly eroded dinosaur tracks. The upriver ends of these prints appear to be divided into the typical three-toed pattern.
>
> A few feet downriver from these is the three-toed dinosaur track-way. These tracks are in a beautiful state of preservation. It appears that if these tracks were eroded down to the

shallowness of the elongated track series near
by, they would look much like the shallow
tracks of the nearby series.[1]

Several comments need to be made about the above
statement. Loma Linda University in Loma Linda,
California, sponsored this work about five years after
the prints were first uncovered. When excavated in
1968 and 1969, the Films for Christ team noted that
these prints were made by bare feet, showing clear toe
marks in several of the tracks. Casts taken at the time
show much more detail than the prints retain now,
and as the river continues to erode them, they will continue to deteriorate.

Evidently the team of investigators did not see all of
the over twenty prints in the trail, nor did they see
any of the other three trails in the same rock shelf or
the fact that three of the four trails cross one or both
of the dinosaur trails. The trail they studied makes
a small angle with one dinosaur trail, and three of the
prints are only inches away from the three-toed tracks.
It crosses the second dinosaur trail at a 60° angle, with
one print again very near the dinosaur trail. Two of
the other trails cross at nearly right angles and one
print actually overlaps a dinosaur track.

These facts are important because the Loma Linda
scientists describe the dinosaur tracks as being in an
excellent state of preservation, while the elongated
tracks are likely the eroded remains of previously
deeper dinosaur tracks. But both the trail with the
three adjacent prints and the trail with the overlapping
print were made after the dinosaur trail! Any erosion
which would have altered the man-like prints would
not have left the dinosaur trail in "an excellent state of
preservation."

Furthermore, not all of the prints in the main sequence are less than one inch deep. Some, in fact, are

This track, print H - 1 + 1 of the Taylor trail, is much too deep to be the middle pad of an eroded dinosaur track.

about four inches deep and these show absolutely no evidence of having once been dinosaur prints.

Other possible explanations have been offered from time to time. Some have thought that since man (according to evolutionary theory) obviously could not have made such a print, they must have been made by an ape. But primates of any sort should not have been around either. Aside from the fact that apes are thought to have evolved only a few tens of millions of years ago, ape feet are not at all like human feet, being more like hands with four fingers and an opposing thumb, and they generally walked on all fours.

Similar problems abound when using the bear as an explanation, another mammal of supposed recent evolutionary origin. Bear feet tend to be much rounder and have long claws. In one place within the Dinosaur Valley State Park, near both man-like and dinosaur prints, there are two unusual prints, more bear-like than anything, and still unidentified. Since the bear is also of much too "recent" origin, the problem is only compounded.

One geologist made the comment that a dolphin brushing up against a mud bank while swimming, can occasionally make an impression with his fin that resembles a human footprint. But again this marine mammal arrives far too late on the evolutionary tree to solve the problem. Furthermore, it is difficult to envision a dolphin making a series of left-right prints with a constant stride, while swimming along a shallow mud flat.

Probably the most likely alternate theory comes from those who suggest that the prints may have been made by a giant forerunner of the modern-day ground sloth. But again according to the evolutionary tree the giant sloth evolved around 40 million years ago and did not arrive in America until about ten million years ago, far too late for a romp with dinosaurs in central Texas.

8-G

Drawings of the foot structure of two sloth skeletons discovered recently. Even though some evolutionists charge that the Paluxy footprints may have been made by such an animal, there is very little similarity between the foot of a ground sloth (nearly 3' long) and a human foot.

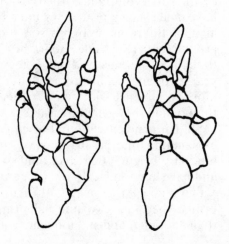

To make matters worse, the giant sloth evidently did not *walk* on his hind legs, but only stood upright for short periods of time, using his tail for support. A quick look at the details of a sloth's foot, possessing huge claws and a radically different toe line, shows little resemblance to a human foot. Furthermore, their feet were commonly a yard in length.

There is one other way in which elongated marks can be made and this possibility has as yet not been conclusively evaluated. Even a casual visitor to Glen Rose will notice that the bottom of the Paluxy River is literally riddled with long ruts that almost everywhere parallel the river flow. In general, these ruts appear in groups of ten or so and seldom merge into one another, ruling out a purely erosional origin.

Some have interpreted these ruts to be dinosaur tail drags, others as "eroded rebound joints." If erosion removes the uppermost part, the back and forth nature can, under certain circumstances, look like a trail of human prints.

Looking along their axis, they have a definite back and forth nature, much like a low amplitude sine curve. In cross section, each rut will show a gradual slope down to the trough on the inside of the curve and a steep to slightly undercut slope on the outside of the curve. The nature of the features in cross section is consistent with the erosional effects of moving water and can be readily seen on a larger scale in meandering streams and rivers.

The big problem as to their origin arises from the fact that adjacent to each rut are places where the rock is higher than the surrounding rock, much like a mud up-push associated with prints. These ruts are sometimes quite deep, up to a foot deep in some places in the Paluxy. They are found only in the layers of rock containing the prints and are generally found when-

The linear ruts in the river bottom can be quite deep. Mike Turnage has one foot on top and the other in the bottom of a rut in the Hondo Creek.

ever prints are found. At the Blanco Creek, 150 miles to the south, dinosaur tracks are found in abundance in the southerly extension of the Glen Rose Limestone, and here again these ruts are found, this time up to three feet deep, but with the same features. Similar ruts have been discovered in many other rivers and creeks where the Glen Rose Limestone forms the river bottom.

Two tentative explanations have been offered, but neither fits all the facts. Mike Turnage, who studied this problem at length, felt that they were made by dinosaurs as they dragged their tails on the bottom while being swept along by a fast-moving current in rather shallow water. The back and forth aspect represented the swimming stroke of the dinosaur trying to fight against being carried away.[2]

The biggest problem with this idea is that the "tail-drags" always seem to follow the flow of the present meandering river. It is conceivable that such ruts could be formed in this way, but one would hardly expect the direction of current at the height of the great Flood to be the same as that of the present-day stream, which may change frequently, even doubling back on itself. But neither is such an explanation feasible in the uniformitarian system, since the present river certainly does not date back to the Cretaceous.

The other possible model, proposed by Baylor University scientists, consists of a more orthodox interpretation, but again does not seem to account for all of the features observed. The ruts which increase in number and depth near the center of the river are thought to be caused by fracturing of the rock due to the removal of the overburden by erosion and regional torsion. Once the crack appeared, it was then scoured out by the moving stream water, obeying normal stream hydrodynamics until its back and forth nature

Rectangular jointing on an exposed shelf of the marker bed. As rebound and erosion take place the rock nearest the joint is raised. This situation may be related to the ruts in the print layer, but their natures are quite different.

was apparent, complete with an undercut and raised lip. In general, this seems the most likely explanation of the ruts.

However, the jointing theory does not fully explain the "up-push" around the edges, it only accommodates them. The Baylor Geologic Survey, in a field guide to the Paluxy, claims: "A feature seen is the peculiar manner in which the joints weather. Near the river the area next to the joints is raised while the center is a depression."[3] Such a cause for the formation of smaller joints with raised lips is observable and unquestioned, but it may be premature to extend such a cause to the larger back and forth ruts.

This author has made a lengthy study of these unusual formations and remains as puzzled as any about their origin. But their origin is not nearly so important as their present-day effect. It seems that if a rut is not too deep, or if erosion has cropped off its top, the remainder can appear to a casual observer to be a trail of "human" prints in a right-left-right-left sequence.

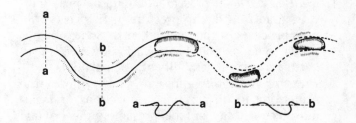

8-K

This "tail drag" or eroded fracture (or whatever it is) can appear under certain circumstances to be a human trail and has been misinterpreted from time to time. Caution is urged.

The lowest part of each rut is usually the point of greatest curvature and so an eroded rut will show a fairly consistent "stride," the natural "straddle" between the "feet," and each "print" will be oriented in the same general direction as the overall "trail."

Of course, the individual "prints" will show no consistent length and will have no features of a human foot other than being elongated with a hint of an arch. They frequently will grade laterally into a typical continuous rut.

Unfortunately, in the past some have mistaken these unusual ruts for man tracks, and pictures of these elongated, featureless ruts have appeared in creationist literature. The following principles of identification are therefore established to avoid unwarranted claims.

Guidelines for distinguishing between normal erosional features and human or animal prints.

1. *Mud up-push*—if present, the mud up-push indicates mud flow due to pressure of foot, except in possible cases of the unusual ruts. Some obvious prints do not exhibit the up-push, however, due to hardness or compactability of original mud.

2. *Pressure striations*—present under most true prints due to differential compactions or metamorphism. May not be present if the original mud is homogeneous, but differential crystallization or metamorphism may provide similar information.

3. *Sequence of prints*—probably the most important feature. Normal erosion cannot produce a right-left-right-left series of prints.

4. *Constant stride*—the prints should be separated by a reasonably constant distance. The stride will vary when changing from a walk to a run.

5. *Constant straddle*—a reasonable lateral separation between right and left should exist.

6. *Directional trend*—the trail should generally trend in one direction, but a change in trend must be allowable.

7. *Trend of individual prints*—each print should also trend in the same general direction as the overall trail.

8. *Size of prints*—the size of the prints should be the same, making allowances for slipping and sliding in the original mud.

9. *Size vs. stride reasonable*—the size of the prints in the series should be reasonable with respect to the stride.

Guidelines for distinguishing between animal prints and true man prints.

10. *Bipedal and upright*—the prints should obviously be that of a two-legged individual, walking upright.

11. *General features of barefoot human foot*—most of the prints should show some of the general features of a human foot and at least one should clearly show enough features to make a diagnosis. The most common features in descending order of occurrence are:

    a. ball of foot
    b. heel
    c. arch
    d. big toe
    e. toe line
    f. toe markings
    g. individual toe depressions
    h. toe ridges

    Furthermore, there should be no evidence that the print was carved or altered in any way to produce the features.

12. *No other animal possible*—be sure that the trail cannot fit any other known animal, and that the clearest prints cannot fit any other animal, such as bear, sloth, or dinosaur.

Guidelines for distinguishing between man tracks and the "tail-drag eroded-joint" linear ruts.

13. *Follow flow of river*—if the markings follow the flow of the river, be suspicious. It is true that many of the man trails are roughly in an east-west trend and may be found in a roughly east-west section of the river, but the strange ruts always follow the river flow. (Downstream from Glen Rose some ruts can be seen going into a low point bar, which appears to have been the river's previous course.)

14. *Grade into obvious joint*—the ruts laterally may grade into an obvious uneroded joint, and if so, then it is not a trail. Many of the ruts have cracks running through them, but this does not rule them out as possible prints.
15. *Grade into a continuous rut*—if the markings increase in length or grade into a continuous rut, then they are not prints.
16. *General feature*—as in guidelines 4, 5, 8, 9, and 11 above, the markings should show the general features of both a human foot and human stride.

All of the above guidelines have known exceptions and as such their application is necessarily subjective. But boiling them down to their essence results in the following statement: **A man trail should be reasonably conformable in sequence and configuration to a modern-day man trail, and at least some of the prints in the trail should contain enough clear features of a man print to rule out nonhuman origin.**

References for Chapter 8

1. Neufeld, Berney, "Dinosaur Tracks and Giant Men," *Origins,* V. 2, No. 2, 1975, p. 70.
2. Turnage, Mike, (unpublished report to ICR), 1971, p. 5.
3. Baylor Geologic Society, Baylor University, Waco, Texas, *Valley of the Giants,* Field Guide, 1973, p. 21.

Chapter 9

The Problem of Carved Tracks

Another type of problem associated with the Paluxy tracks is whether the prints may in fact be carvings and not real footprints at all. Undoubtedly this contention has some basis in fact, for back in the thirties, once the best specimens had been removed from the river bottom and sold, a few enterprising Texans from Glen Rose began to copy the originals on limestone chunks and then to offer these forgeries for sale also.

The going price for prints ranged from $10 to $50, and since the dinosaur prints were much more in demand, they brought the highest price. Evidently dozens of dinosaur tracks were carved, but as near as the researchers can determine, only a very few "man tracks" were carved, probably no more than six, certainly less than ten. These were all giant tracks, ranging from 16 to 20 inches in length and showed all the features of a human foot.

These counterfeit tracks do not, of course, disprove the genuine tracks. A counterfeit usually implies an original. In fact, it could only have been the reported

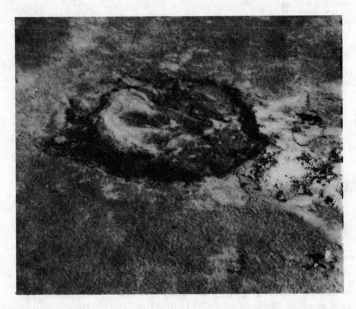

During the depression some of the prints were chiseled from the river and sold. This dinosaur print was only partially excavated when abandoned.

existence of genuine tracks that made the manufacture of counterfeits profitable.

As far as is known, only one man carved any man prints at all. Mr. George Adams, the local mailman, was known as a practical joker and smooth operator. Some of the old timers still remember how he could make a "genuine" Indian arrowhead in a matter of minutes.

At the conference in Glen Rose on Thanksgiving weekend in 1970 (described in Chapter 2), Wayland "Slim" Adams, nephew of George Adams, stood before the gathering of Ph.D.'s and explained how his uncle had carved the prints. It may have been easier to carve a track out of a suitable limestone block than to extract one intact from the stratum. Mike Turnage was present and retells Adam's story:

The technique involved first finding a suitable-sized stone that contained natural dips for the ball and heel. Next a cool area under a spreading oak was selected as the workshop. With hammer and chisel, skilled hands could produce a track (dinosaur or human) complete in all details. Some carved "human" tracks were produced in giant sizes. A center-punch might be used to produce raindrops in the track. Now the problem was to remove the chisel marks. This was easily done with muriatic acid. Aging was accomplished by covering the carving with manure and letting it rest for a few days in a cool place. When washed off, the edges were chipped to give the impression

Fake or carved prints, such as this one near Alex, Oklahoma, have an unnatural appearance, very little relief, and certainly no up-push or subsurface signs.

of an old stained track newly removed from the bedrock.[1]

There are no written records, of course, but evidently not too many prints were carved. No one else is known to have carved any, and according to friends and relatives, George Adams carved only a very few. Mr. Carroll Hulsey, long-time resident of Glen Rose, claimed that to the best of his knowledge, Adams had carved only two man tracks, and Mrs. Stone, Adam's daughter, felt that her father had carved only one. Both remembered that he had carved many dinosaur tracks, however. Slim Adams relates this story about one carved "human" track:

> News [of the track] reached a Dallas or Fort Worth newspaper, and somehow it came to the attention of the Smithsonian Institution. The Smithsonian Institution wired that they had men already on the way to Glen Rose to examine the track which they thought to be a real one. Ernest Tolbert (Bull) Adams, the brilliant lawyer and archaeologist of Glen Rose, told George Adams to disappear for two weeks and not to be found until the men from the Smithsonian had left. He also told him to get rid of or to bury that track. And so he buried the track. When the men from the Smithsonian arrived, George Adams could not be found and after looking fruitlessly for two weeks, they finally left without having seen either the track or Adams. The track supposedly passed through a few hands. Finally it was bought for a sum of $20-25 by Bob Gentry.[2]

The man-like track was purported to have been found on the property of Mrs. Stone (daughter of the carver) and bought first by Mr Hulsey who sold it eventually to Gentry on behalf of Columbia Union

Footprints carved onto "Newspaper Rock" in the Petrified Forest in New Mexico.

College in Maryland. The track itself was of inferior quality with short stubby toes. The little toe was curled underneath as if the person had been wearing shoes all his life. In recent years the track has been analyzed in the laboratory. The banding in the rock showed no deformation at all, and all agree that it is a carving.

There is some scanty hearsay evidence collected by Clifford Burdick that another fake track (possibly two) was sold to two California construction workers as they passed through Glen Rose, but, of course, there is no record.

Wayland Adams tells another interesting story, this one about his father Bull Adams. Educated at Oxford, Bull Adams had returned to his native Glen Rose to become a dynamic, but somewhat eccentric community leader. He had played a major role in the removal of the brontosaur trail for the Natural History Museum in New York. According to Charlie Moss, Bull Adams had been the first to discover the now destroyed trail of well-preserved man tracks in 1908. He had also promoted the coexistence of man and dinosaur tracks in the Glen Rose area, and documentation of his new proposed species "Texanus Gargantuas" appeared in many newspapers touted as a prehistoric giant human. Eventually, however, the curiosity seekers began to bother him. In order to stop the flow of tourists into what then was a quiet, mineral springs resort area, he ordered the local merchants to pass the word that all of the human tracks were fakes.

When considering the human-like prints which are not now in the riverbed (and therefore possible carvings), there remains even now a lack of agreement. As mentioned previously, the first ones to surface were seen by Roland Bird in Gallup, New Mexico, and subsequently pictures of them appeared in *The Genesis Flood*. They had reportedly been secured by Al Berry and Jack Hill in 1938 from Glen Rose. Berry's certified statement was quoted in Chapter 2. Further information is provided in this letter to Dr. Burdick from Eryl Cummings: "I personally knew Al Berry for years. In fact, I considered him a good friend. I can only say he was honest in all his business dealings with my real estate office. Here is the story as Al told it to me:"

> While owner of a trading post located on Highway 66 near Gallup, New Mexico, a friend dropped in to tell him about human and dinosaur tracks he had seen in the bed of the Paluxy River. The friend explained that work was being done in the area with heavy equipment and that the tracks might be marred or destroyed. Al Berry and his friend decided to act immediately. The following morning, according to

Al, they were in Glen Rose. Arrangements were made with one of the men with an air compressor and jack hammer to cut out the blocks of track containing the footprints. The footprints were taken from the riverbed and transported in their car to Gallup.

In recent years the tracks were purchased by Bob Gentry on behalf of Columbia Union College. In a personal letter to Dr. H. M. Morris at the Institute for Creation Research, dated July 5, 1971, he writes:

It is my considered opinion after several years of work that the giant human footprints at one time certainly did exist in the riverbed of the Paluxy River. About this point I have no question. However, I do have a question as to whether or not the tracks which are at Columbia Union College are actually authentic. I did not have these doubts two or three years ago, but the information that has come to me in the meantime gives me reason to believe that several people may have been engaged in a conspiracy to produce these tracks for monetary gain. I think it is entirely possible that George Adams may have fabricated the tracks in the bed of the Paluxy River and subsequently called in a group of trading post collectors. To those who were unsuspecting, this would have given the appearance of the tracks having been found as were the dinosaur tracks. In any event, the affidavit which Mr. Berry gave to Eryl Cummings may very well be true as far as the information he had. They were excavated from the bed of the Paluxy River, but there is some question as to whether or not George Adams did not actually carve them there before Mr. Berry was called in. I think we must maintain the position that the tracks now at Columbia Union College may very well be spurious ones.

In hopes of settling the issue once and for all, Dr. Don Jones of Columbia Union College subjected one of the dinosaur tracks, one of Berry's man-like tracks, and Gentry's man-like print, purchased at Glen Rose and known to be a fake, to laboratory tests. These prints were all sawn open in strategic spots to determine if lines of discoloration or banding in the limestone were depressed, as discussed in the previous chapter. The fake print was obviously a fake print, as was the dinosaur print. But some disagreement still remains about the detailed man-like print purchased from Al Berry.[3]

The problem arises due to the fact that the mud was quite homogeneous (without noticeable banding), at the time the mud hardened into rock. A footprint in such mud would therefore produce no depressed laminations, since *no* laminations were there. Scientists from Columbia Union College, by examining the grain structure of the rock under magnification, concluded that the print had nothing in common with the rock matrix and was, therefore, a carving.

Dr. Burdick, however, disagreed. He noted that the rock appeared yellowish due to small bits of iron present in the original mud. When the sectioned end of the track was moistened, the portion directly under the print—and only that section—changed color and took on a mottled appearance. According to Dr. Burdick:

I personally observed the sectioned track, and found evidence of definite pressure in the form of incipient metamorphism, that is, whereas the whole slab of limestone was buff in color, the area directly beneath the foot was white, due to recrystallizing the limestone into

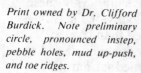

Print owned by Dr. Clifford Burdick. Note preliminary circle, pronounced instep, pebble holes, mud up-push, and toe ridges.

white calcite, leaving the coloring impurities behind. This recrystallization was apparently due to pressure from above, that is, the weight of the man.[4]

And so the issue is not yet settled. Most researchers tend to feel that the print is a carving, but some who have seen the white calcite crystallization beneath the track are of the opinion that the track is genuine.

The next most important set of tracks is owned by Clifford Burdick himself and consist of a man-like track and a large cat track. Burdick purchased the man print from a Rev. Beddoe of Arizona. Beddoe had in turn purchased it years ago from the late Peesee Hudson, who had operated a knick-knack type store in Glen Rose. Many things had been sold in that store, including some of George Adam's carvings. Tracing the print proved impossible, but it was purported to have come from a tributary of the Paluxy, south of Glen Rose.

Again, most researchers feel that Burdick's track is a carving. Sawing the print in half did not solve the problem either. The work was done at Loma Linda University and it was reported that:

> The evidence is equivocal. Some cross sections give a slight indication of carving, others of conformation. The difficulty with these tracks is that they are in blocks of limestone whose pattern is more mottled than layered.[5]

Other scientists are more certain, including Burdick:

> When my track was sectioned at Loma Linda University, the same phenomena of white calcite crystals showed up, though not quite as prominently as in the case of the Berry tracks.[6]

Doyle Cooper, a Texas A & M agriculturist, who lived in Glen Rose for twenty-five years, signed the following document when shown a cast of Dr. Bur-

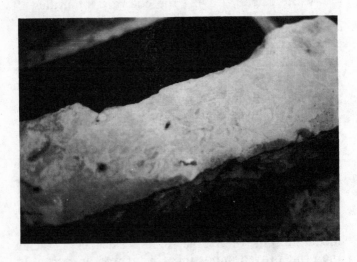

The mottled nature underneath Burdick's track is seen here. Note that the mottled effect is more pronounced directly under the print than elsewhere.

dick's print in August, 1969:

> This track is definitely not the track I saw a
> man make here in the late forties or early fif-
> ties. I watched this man [Adams] make a
> track, but it had stubby toes and was wider in
> comparison to the length. The thing I remem-
> ber was the man said he was making a replica
> of one that had been dug up. None of the pic-
> tures you showed me of man tracks were ones
> that had been carved. The rock the carver had
> was more yellow and harder, an upland rock
> and hexagonal rather than oval as the pictures
> you showed me.

According to Jim Ryals, Slim Adams, and others,
all prints removed from the river were nearly circular,
generally having been torqued free from the underlying rock. Carvings could have been made from any
shape rock, although once removed from the river, a
slab could have been trimmed to lessen the weight.
The Berry tracks are rather rectangular, while Burdick's track is nearly circular.

Jim Ryals, who had been responsible for removal
of most of the tracks from the river, claimed that although he had removed at least one better track, he
had not removed Burdick's track. He was uncertain
about its authenticity, but pointed out that he always
allowed more room around the outside of the track to
avoid cracking the rock. In fact, when carving either
dinosaur or man prints, artificial rain drops or pock
marks would be punched into the surface of the rock
and print, but never within an inch or so of the edge,
again to avoid cracking.

A joint study of the print by Dr. George Westcott,
an anatomist, and Dr. Burdick yielded the following
points which serve not as a firm proof as to its genuineness, but as presumptive evidence.[7]

Close up of toe area of Burdick's track.

Close up of heel area of Burdick's track.

1. Dr. Westcott had made two barefoot impressions in plaster for comparison, one while standing still which turned out almost flat, and the other while walking, which had a deeper impression for the ball of the foot. The Burdick track has such an impression.

2. In the walking plaster impression and in Burdick's track the highest point anywhere turned out to be the separation between the big toe and the next toe, as is true on Burdick's track, where one can rock a straightedge across the ridge. This would be nearly impossible to carve.

3. There is a shallow preliminary circle around the track, as if the remover began to cut at that point, but enlarged the circle to lessen the possibilities of damage to the track. In a carving, such a preliminary line would not be necessary.

4. The print has a pronounced instep. Comparison of this print with the known Glen Rose carving and with the numerous carved prints from different sources around the country, reveals that none of the others has an arch.

5. There are no chisel marks on the print.

6. The track surface has several little round holes where pebbles have been. One such hole in the heel has been flattened by pressure and the mud rolled back before hardening.

7. Just behind the heel a little lip or roll of former mud appears to have been pushed back by the pressure of the heel.

8. Distinct mud up-push formations are visible behind the heel and on the right side of the track.

9. Iron Oxide lines, evidently caused by pressure, show up all over the face of the track.

10. As mentioned before, a slight line of metamorphism or change in crystallization can be seen in

a cross section, roughly following the contour of the toe and ball of the foot. Below the entire print the mottled metamorphism is evident, but to a much greater degree than that a few inches away from the print.

It seems that the only negative aspects of Burdick's print are that it cannot be traced to a specific location on the Paluxy, its past ownership is uncertain, the cross section was not definitive, and—perhaps most important—it is just too good. None of the prints in the river bed are nearly as distinct.

Large cat track also reported to be found in Glen Rose Limestone. Such cats are thought by evolutionists to have evolved about 50 million years ago—not 120 million years ago, which is the age they have placed on the rock.
Photo by Burdick.

Burdick's cat track, when it was sectioned, possessed much better striations under the print than did the man track, although the rock was also somewhat mottled. There seems little doubt that it is a genuine print. Large cats such as this are thought to have evolved in the middle Tertiary period—or about 50 million years ago. This is still quite different than the 100 to 120-million-year age assigned to the Glen Rose strata, and therefore is almost as damaging to evolution theory.

Sectioning of the cat track proved its authenticity. Depressed laminations paralleling the contour of the cat's paw prove that it was not carved.

The other man-like print that is available for observation sits in the yard of the Gibbs Sanitarium in downtown Glen Rose. Similar in size and detail to the

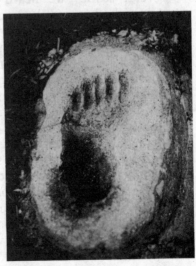

This man-like print on display at the Gibbs Sanitarium in Glen Rose was covered with concrete once it began to erode. It may be a carved print, but has never been sectioned for analysis.

other prints discussed above, it has been almost completely disregarded by researchers, and with good reason, because about fifteen years after they had acquired it, the track had weathered so badly that the owners attempted to repair it with cement.

The print reportedly had been removed from the riverbed by Mr. L. R. Parvin of Fort Worth and his father. They claim to have found it in a limestone wash south of Glen Rose and sold it to Dr. Gibbs in Glen Rose. Dr. Burdick saw the print first in the early 1950's soon after it had been removed, and it was in fine shape. He recorded the story in personal interviews with the Parvins. By the early 1960's the print had weathered badly, and in 1966 the sanitarium recovered it with cement. Stan Taylor began his investigation in 1968. Later he wrote:

> Charlie Moss showed us a dry stream bed in a field outside Glen Rose where he said the track had been cut out of the rock. One of several stories we heard was that George Adams had carved the track in the stone surface of the dry creek and then later the Parvins came upon it and dug it out.[8]

No further investigations have been carried out at this location due to the suspicious nature of the print. But something else is suspicious here. George Adams had evidently made a tidy sum of money selling his fake dinosaur tracks. In fact, he had a regular business going. But if he carved this print, he did so out in a dry stream bed on someone else's land, abandoned it there, only to have it found and removed by someone else. Adams did not get paid for this job, and, indeed, if he was foolish enough to carve such a print in the creek bed instead of under a nice shade tree, and then leave it there, he did not deserve either the money or his reputation as a clever dealer.

The story is quite similar to the one Bob Gentry tells about the prints purchased by Columbia Union College from Al Berry. Berry "discovered" the prints in the river bottom near a construction site. The jackhammer operator had already removed about ten of the prints for himself and was hired by Berry and Jack Hill to remove some for them. If George Adams had carved these prints, spread the word to trading post operators as related to Gentry, and had the local construction crew fooled into thinking they were genuine, then he also fooled himself, for he was not there to collect. It may be true. Adams may have carved the prints in the riverbed. There must have been a total of about twenty, including dinosaur, man, and large cats. He may indeed have left them there in downtown Glen Rose, about 300 feet from the largest hotel in town, and not been there to collect when the buyers came in. Anything is possible. But since the cross sections do not settle the issue, and the testimonies indicate that they were removed intact from the river, it may be easier to believe they are genuine prints and that the fabrication is in the story, not in the rock.

This chapter must conclude with the acknowledgment that none of the tracks which have been removed from the riverbed, whether they be real or fake, are sufficient to prove that man and dinosaurs walked together at Glen Rose. Tracks in place are of much greater value than samples whose origins cannot be well authenticated. Actually, the usefulness of any print is compromised once it is removed.

It is both disconcerting and encouraging that there are so many stories about near-perfect man tracks found in the Paluxy in the past. Some were removed, some were eroded, some were lost, and some were copied. Unfortunately, these excellent prints are far superior in quality to all known prints now in the riverbed. The conclusion is obvious. If there were real prints in the past that distinctly showed all the features of the human foot, there may be more buried under the other layers. Someday they may be found and all doubts will be put to rest.

Now, however, we do have many man-like tracks, still in the river bed, which could not possibly have been carved by George Adams or anyone else. They are not perfect footprints, but they do seem sufficiently good to make a positive identification.

References for Chapter 9

1. Turnage, Mike, (unpublished report to ICR), 1971, p.5
2. *Ibid.*, pp. 4, 5.
3. Neufeld, Berney, "Dinosaur Tracks and Giant Men," *Origins,* V. 2, No. 2.
4. Burdick, Clifford, *Adventures in Geology* (unpublished manuscript).
5. Neufeld, pp. 74, 75.
6. Burdick, Clifford, "Letter to the Editor," *Origins,* V. 3, No. 1, 1976, p. 8.
7. *Ibid.*
8. Taylor, Stanley A., "Mystery Tracks in Dinosaur Valley," *Bible Science Newsletter,* April, 1971, p. 2.

Chapter 10

Location of
All Known Trails

All too often one hears the statement, "My family and I went to Glen Rose to see the man prints, but couldn't find any. We asked the park rangers, but they just laughed and said there were none, and that man prints were carvings."

This is very disappointing to one who has spent years studying the prints. The evidence does exist and is worth seeing. It would be better if many people could see and photograph the prints, and then tell others. News of the prints and their implication would be disseminated much faster.

It is a fact that few of the prints are readily visible without excavating the riverbank or at least sandbagging off an area. But many people would be willing to do a little work if they just knew where. In addition, several fairly good prints are exposed and quite accessible, but again, if one did not know where to look, the prints would be difficult to find.

A real danger exists, however, in publishing the locations of the prints. In this day and age there seem to be many individuals with twisted minds who love to deface or destroy anything of value to another, seemingly with no motive at all. There are others who would do the same thing without hesitation if they had a motive. The existence of evidence that man and dinosaur lived at the same time—in obvious violation of the concept of evolution—might provide sufficient motive to some ardent evolutionists.

AERIAL PHOTO OF PALUXY RIVER

Once when the author was talking on this subject in a high school assembly, for example, the head science teacher began beating on the table in front of him with his shoe and yelled incoherent statements and vile oaths, much to the delight of the student body. On another occasion at a major university an anthropology professor threw a folding chair across the room when confronted with the evidence. It is true that many scientists and laymen alike cannot and do not keep an open mind when the faith to which they are committed is challenged.

But despite the risks involved in publishing the location of these prints, it must be done. This chapter will take the form of a survey of the Paluxy, as if one were to start walking downstream several miles upstream from Glen Rose with broom and shovel and elbow grease, noting all interesting features. These features include geographic landmarks, geologic markers such as prominent outcrop or fossil layers, and, of course, the footprints, both human and dinosaur. The locations are marked on the accompanying map so that their relocation by others will be easier.

Such a survey was carried out in July and August of 1977 by Dale Murphy, Fernando Guilarte, and the author. The material presented here, however, is a compilation of all known information that has come to the author's attention. Other trails may exist, but no others are known that are of any significance.

The more significant human trails are described and documented in detail in the Appendix. Primarily, only the location and a brief description of these trails will be given in this chapter; hopefully, overlap has been kept to a minimum.

Point 1 (Fifth Crossing)

We begin our survey at what is known as the fifth

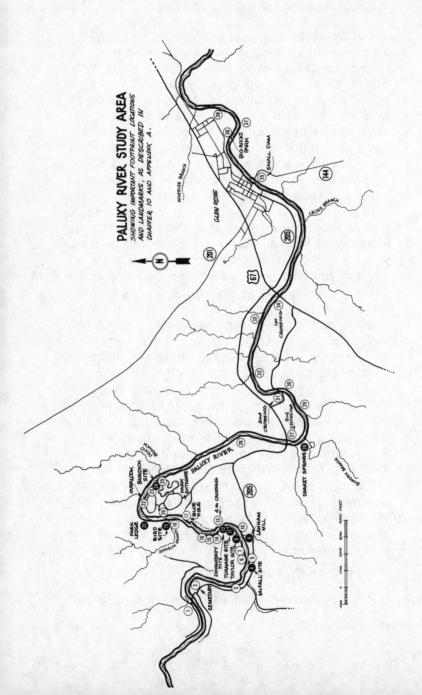

crossing where a ford in the river provides access to a Girl Scout Camp from State Highway 205. Upstream of this ford, which is referred to as Point 1 on the map, no prints of any sort have been reported.

Point 2 (Cemetery)

Walking downstream we pass the Lanham Mill Cemetery on the right bank. Although the cemetery is currently in use, it contains some very old and interesting gravestones. The river bends to the right at this point, and under normal conditions the water is quite deep and still.

The river bottom in most places is covered with over two feet of mud and the riverbanks are badly eroded and foliated. No prints or outcrops are visible.

Point 3 (Highway 205) — See Appendix

Approximately one-half mile downstream, Highway 205 closely parallels the stream bank and as the river bends to the left, a limestone shelf has been used as the road surface. This "marker bed" is approximately 6-10 inches thick throughout much of the Glen Rose area and is useful in locating the layers which are known to contain prints. The layer is almost free of fossils that are visible to the unaided eye and is very hard and resistant to erosion. Where it has broken away, a layer of blue-gray claystone lies underneath, generally 12-30 inches thick. The layer of limestone beneath the clay layer varies in hardness, color, resistance to erosion, texture, fossil content, and thickness from place to place, but it is that bed that contains almost all of the known tracks. Surprisingly, even though the print layer is much more easily eroded than the more resistant limestone marker bed, it forms the river bottom throughout most of the area, with the broken edge of the marker bed visible on the banks.

The marker bed, when finally broken and the intervening clay layer eroded, reveals the main print layer. Previously it was possible to remove this layer with heavy equipment, but recent state regulations have made it illegal.

Dr. Dougherty has located a series of four indentations on the marker bed here, but they are unconvincing at best.

Point 4 (McFall Site) — See Appendix

Continuing downstream for about one-fourth mile, on the right bank lies a series of 14 tracks which Emmett McFall has shown to tourists for years (for a small fee). They are large and badly eroded and are unrecognizable, although many have made the claim that they were made by human feet wearing a covering or moccasin. This site has been called the McFall site by some and Site 1 by Wilbur Fields. Two obvious dinosaur trails cross the eroded trail and another eroded dinosaur trail can be seen on a ledge in the center of the river.

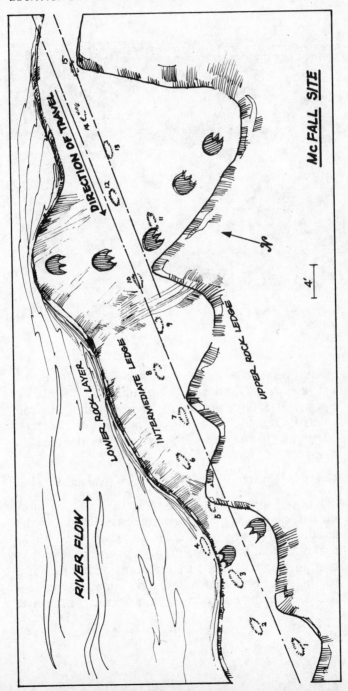

McFALL SITE

McFall site. Here Emmett McFall has shown a series of 14 badly eroded prints. Fernando Guilarte indicates the location of the trail.

On close examination, these prints have slender toe or claw marks similar to those studied at the Shakey Springs Site, discussed later. They should not be considered human. The beast that had such an elongated foot with slender toes is not known, but it was not a human.

Point 5 (Elevated Print Layer) — See Appendix

Not far downstream are a series of about ten dinosaur tracks and six large man-like tracks on a ledge about five feet above water level. It is difficult to determine if that layer is the usual print layer due to river bottom mud and lack of continuous outcrops, but if so, this is the only print location for some distance that is above normal water level. In the center of the river

One of the impressions at the McFall site that have at times been mistaken for human prints.

Park Ledge. One of the most popular tourist sites. Adjacent to and down stream from the ledge are both brontosaur and tyrannosaur tracks. Several man-like trails and numerous other tracks, as well as bear-like tracks and poorly preserved dinosaur tracks, are visible on the ledge (Point 21).

© *FFC. Photo by Taylor.*

are several man-like impressions that are not in any particular trail. They are rather indistinct and since they are normally covered by deep water and gravel, they have never been carefully studied.

Point 6 (Ware Prints) — See Appendix

In 1971, Turnage and crew found numerous possible trails and prints in an area usually covered by deep water. The prints were eroded and indistinct, but perhaps give promise of future success as the nearby banks are excavated.

Point 7 (Moss Trail) — See Appendix

Further downriver is the location on the left bank of the river where Charlie Moss and Bull Adams had seen the well-preserved man tracks washed away in 1918. Almost directly across the river at this point on the McFall side of the river, four elongated tracks are seen in stride going directly upstream to the point where the ledge breaks off. However, these lack sufficient definition.

Point 8 (Lanham Mill) — See Appendix

Immediately adjacent to Emmett McFall's home, the remains of the old Lanham Mill still stand. McFall owns this property and on occasions he has allowed fishermen and footprint work crews to park there. This place is ideal for parking, only about 50 feet from the river and within 200 yards of many of the most important man trails. The river is reached by crawling through a hole in the fence and walking down a narrow path through the underbrush (lined with terrifying "bull nettles"). Here a barbed wire fence has been strung across the river.

Just a few yards downstream from the fence are several interesting tracks, but the most interesting is a

This hole marks the spot where a slab containing both human and dinosaur tracks were reportedly removed. Four raised dinosaur tracks remain in stride with the hole, but the elongated tracks (man-like) are near the river bank.

"missing" track, a large circular hole in the rock where Jim Ryals claims to have removed a slab of rock containing both a human and dinosaur track. To be sure, one dinosaur track leads into the hole and three leave it. As for the man tracks, they are thought to be moccasin prints by some and are quite large. They are very near the shoreline and usually covered with debris, and it seems unlikely that one of them could have been included in the cut out.

The dinosaur tracks here at Point 8 are quite interesting. They are of the three-toed variety, but differ from most of the other prints in that they are inverted or raised, instead of being impressions in the rock. Evidently the mud squeezed back into each print after it had been made, or perhaps they were made after the initial layer of overlying mud had been deposited, but at any rate, the prints are raised and rather indis-

This unique dinosaur mold, an inverted footprint was found near the 4th crossing. It is not merely a raised print as one also found nearby, but part of the underlying rock. (The middle toe of the dinosaur print is near the man's right foot.) (Point 14.)

tinct. The moccasin prints are not raised, but are the usual depressions.

Point 9 (Taylor Site) — See Appendix

Not far downstream Jacob McFall had once dug out a barefoot man track in an area now covered with sand and rock. A few prints are upstream of the hole, but many are downstream. The trail fades in and out —evidently due to inconsistency of the original mud or pools of water, etc. It is this area, however, that has received the most attention. The downstream extension of this trail was first excavated by Stanley Taylor

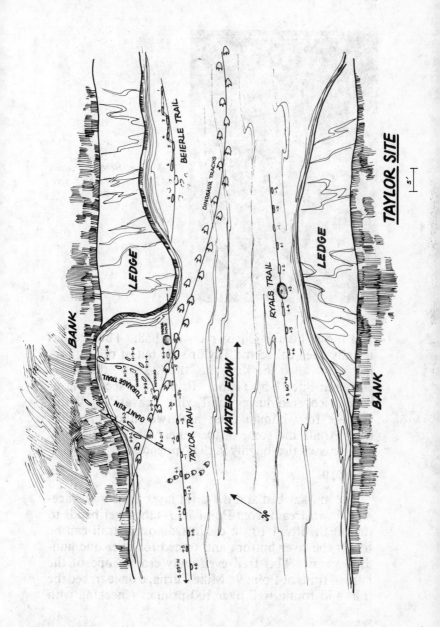

TAYLOR SITE

Taylor Site. Here 4 man trails and 2 dinosaur trails intersect.

and the Films for Christ crew in 1968. The site has usually been called the Taylor site, but at other times has been called the Kerr site, the K-3 site, the movie site, and Site II by Fields. Prints in a second layer were discovered during the Taylor excavation. At this site are four human trails and two dinosaur trails. These trails and some of the others already listed will be discussed thoroughly in the Appendix.

Point 10

The marker bed and the print layer are easily trace-able downstream from Point 7. As the river bends to the north (Point 10), a distinct dinosaur trail can be felt in the river bottom and traced for over one hundred yards. This trail eventually crosses one of the human trails at Point 9. Mike Turnage once traced the trail and found well over 100 prints. Checking with the American Museum of Natural History, this trail is much longer than the longest trail on record. Turnage felt that this dinosaur trail was well worth fully documenting to establish a new record and call attention to the site. As the river bends, the water is generally quite deep, and sandbagging to document the dinosaur trail might reveal some additional human prints, since two of the human trails at Point 9 originate from that direction.

On the far end of the curve, numerous broken slabs of rock lie strewn about. Here is where Charlie Moss feels his 1908 trail was redeposited.

As the river straightens out and heads north, the water depth lessens and numerous dinosaur trails can be seen. Some are solitary prints not associated with a trail, indicating perhaps that isolated puddles in the original mud were of the proper consistency to pre-

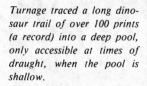

Turnage traced a long dinosaur trail of over 100 prints (a record) into a deep pool, only accessible at times of draught, when the pool is shallow.

serve prints. Here, too, are more of the strange raised prints.

Point 11 (Turnage Site) — See Appendix

Below the end of the long dinosaur trail the left (west) bank of the river contains some elongated prints which look more man-like than anything. Turnage and crew studied these prints carefully in June, 1972, before deciding that they were too inclusive and should not be used as evidence. The prints disappear under about four feet of sand and debris, and excavation did not reveal more. The rubble covers the print layer for about 100 yards and is about 20 feet wide. This would be an excellent place to excavate, since it would not require the use of any major equipment, just lots of hard work, although the rubble covers a previous location of the river, and the print layer may be eroded.

Turnage Site. Mike Turnage and Tom Henderson excavated and studied a trail of man-like tracks which did not show sufficient markings to establish their origin with certainty.

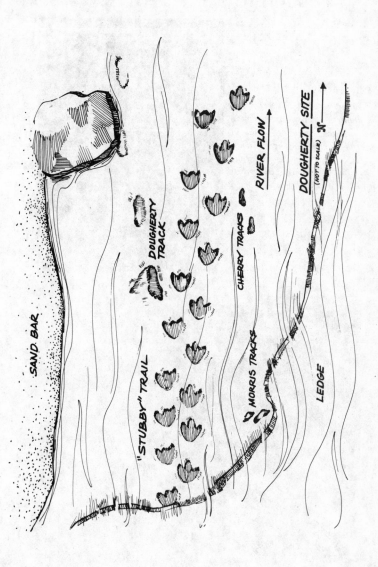

SAND BAR

DOUGHERTY TRACK

"STUBBY" TRAIL

CHERRY TRACKS

MORRIS TRACKS

RIVER FLOW

DOUGHERTY SITE
(NOT TO SCALE)

N

LEDGE

Dougherty Site. Several good man prints have been found here near a good dinosaur trail. The Dougherty Print, a large partially indistinct print, has been questioned by many investigators.

Without outlining the Dougherty print with water, it is not nearly as visible.

Point 12 (Dougherty Site) — See Appendix

Less than 100 yards downstream where the marker bed forms a ledge all the way across the river creating a beautiful waterfall, Dr. Dougherty, a local chiropractor, has found his "Dougherty trail." These three giant prints are immediately adjacent to a well-preserved dinosaur trail. Opinions are many and varied concerning the authenticity of the find, but the prints are of the same general size as other giant prints in the area. Mike Turnage and Tom Henderson feel that the main print is actually one-half of a poorly formed dinosaur print with the "third and fourth toes" scratched into the limestone with a sharp instrument. Nevertheless, there are three of the prints (perhaps five) in a

This print is called the Morris print and when first discovered was in a state of excellent preservation.

right-left sequence of fairly constant stride, although all are rather eroded.

Furthermore, this location, called the "Dougherty site" and now Point 12, has yielded other prints which are much more distinct and certain. One trail of several prints, called the Cherry trail, contained prints of about nine inches long. Perhaps the most perfect print found in recent years was discovered in October of 1975 by the author and Drs. Blick and Dougherty right at the edge of the little waterfall in an area recently exposed by the cracking off of a section of the marker bed. This print was about 13 inches long and showed all the features of the foot clearly. Unfortunately, the previous print had been eroded by the waterfall action and the next one would have been under the ledge. When we next returned to the site in July of 1976, the waterfall had already eroded this print almost beyond recognition.

Point 13 (Fourth Crossing)

North of Point 12 is the abondoned "fourth crossing." In years past this crossing made access to the Taylor site and many of the nearby farms much easier, but the park has now closed this ford and all that remains of the road is an overgrown path.

There has been some misunderstanding about the fourth crossing. In Roland Bird's articles about his discoveries, he claimed that the series of prints seen by Charlie Moss and others back before 1918 were at the fourth crossing. This is not true. In fact, while his articles are informative and make delightful reading, many of the details reported were evidently for literary purposes and not intended for documentation. This is seen by a careful comparison of his two main articles and more easily seen when one has a working knowledge of the river and the people involved.

Some very good dinosaur prints are visible at low water near the abandoned 4th crossing.

Numerous dinosaur tracks and unidentifiable markings cover the river bottom for some distance below the crossing. These can rarely be seen, except when the river is dry.

Point 14

Continuing downstream in a northerly direction, a most unique formation has been discovered. On the top of a large slab of rock on the left bank of the river rests a limestone "mold" of a small dinosaur print. The block is not attached to any layer, but the inverted print is pointed upward—not downward, as it must have originally been, and there is no reason to think that the slab is now upside down. Although several possible mechanisms could have formed the cast, all are highly unlikely and certainty is impossible.

Slim Adams found similar formations on the bottom of a limestone ledge while digging a pond nearby. One such mold is very human in shape.

When Slim Adams was digging a pond on his farm near the Brazos River, he found numerous prints in the mud below a limestone shelf (above and left).

Point 15

There is a slight, but noticeable change in dip of the strata here, as seen in the bank outcrops.

Point 16

Soon after the change in dip, the marker bed thins and finally disappears. It is replaced by a thin conglomerate layer of rounded stones and then by a thickening layer of clay which contains seemingly millions of fossil clams. These clams are important in understanding the deposition of the layers. They are found so closely packed that this could not have been a normal living environment for them. Furthermore, they are usually found with both sides tightly clamped together. Since a clam relaxes its muscles upon death, opening its shell, it is obvious that these were buried alive by some sort of catastrophe. The water action collected and buried them in the position in which they are found.

Point 17 (Blue Hole)

One of the main attractions at the state park is the Blue Hole, where swimming is popular. Just upstream from the Blue Hole are several mediocre dinosaur tracks, but downstream are several types of tracks in an excellent state of preservation. The water at this point is generally quite deep, and it is impossible to study the strata thoroughly, but by following the rubble and fossil layer, it is fairly certain that the tracks are in the same layer as before. There are indications, however, that prints are in more than one layer.

Some very interesting markings have been discovered from time to time near the Blue Hole. Just upstream Mike Turnage and Slim Adams photographed and documented a unique print which evidently was

The Blue Hole. A deep hole just right for swimming after a day of print hunting in the hot Texas sun.

the front paw of a bipedal dinosaur. It had several "fingers" and on first glance looked like the print of a large human hand. Nearby, Bull Adams had discovered a trail of large (approximately 21") elongated tracks which had a stride of nearly seven feet. They very nearly matched several trails of large human-like prints found throughout the area. The trail disappeared near the Blue Hole, but a similar trail could be found near the place where Roland Bird removed the large slabs. The elder Adams had published his findings in a Dallas newspaper, claiming the prints were made by "Texanus gargantuas," a race of giant humans living in the Cretaceous Period.

The main print layer here is only a few inches thick. Many of the prints go all the way through the limestone into a layer of clay below. This is extremely important evidence for rapid deposition of the carbonate sediments followed quickly by the footprints.

About 20 feet above the print layer is a layer of rock, composed primarily of crushed fossils in a lime matric, called the Thorp Spring member of the Glen Rose Limestone. The surface weathers and looks much darker than most of the other rock in the area. This bed has been removed by erosion except in the park, where it forms the high hills. It also remains downstream of Glen Rose in Big Rocks City Park.

Numerous dinosaur prints can be seen near the Blue Hole. They are in a thin limestone layer, so thin that the prints go through it into a clay layer below.

Point 18 (Oppossum Branch)

Downstream from the Blue Hole the layers are quite difficult to follow. Dinosaur prints are found in a layer above the fossil layer near Oppossum Branch.

Point 19 (Bird Excavation)

Roland Bird removed his series of sauropod tracks

Clear dinosaur prints found near the Blue Hole.

near an abandoned river crossing. When he did his work, prints of several sorts were clear and numerous, but now the print layer is eroded and missing in places, with many of the prints unclear. Slim Adams and other Glen Rose residents clearly remember a trail of giant human tracks diagonally crossing Bird's excavation area.

Point 20 (Fields Site)

Wilbur Fields and friends discovered and documented three lengthy sauropod trails in the riverbed, seen for the first time when the river was completely dry. Quite possibly they are the downstream extension of the Bird series and are adjacent to the park picnic

Newly-exposed Brontosaurus trail in the Paluxy River limestone bed. Note inward slope of bottom of feet, and mud pushups beside tracks. The trail is by the east bank of the Paluxy in Dinosaur Valley State Park, a hundred yards south of the crossing area. View SW. Photo July, 1978, by Wilbur Fields.

pavillion. These trails have not been promoted by the park personnel, although they would be welcome additions to presently inadequate and eroding exhibits. They could be permanently exposed and preserved quite easily and would no doubt become the main attraction in the park.

Point 21 (Park Ledge) — See Appendix

Currently the most important and best visited site in the park is the place where two clear brontosaur tracks can be seen just at the edge of an overhanging ledge. These two prints trend in the same direction as the three trails at the Fields site and as the Bird series, and may in fact be the downstream extension of one of them. Nearby are some large tyrannosaur tracks and also other three-toed types, but all have been exposed

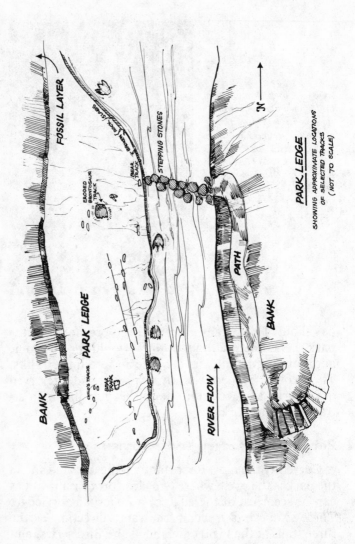

FOSSIL LAYER

ERODED ROCK CLUMPS

ERODED BRONTOSAUR TRACK

BEAR TRACK

STEPPING STONES

N

PARK LEDGE

PATH

BANK

PARK LEDGE

CHILD'S TRACKS

BEAR TRACK

RIVER FLOW

BANK

PARK LEDGE

SHOWING APPROXIMATE LOCATIONS
OF SELECTED TRACKS
(NOT TO SCALE)

*The most accessible of sites where human tracks can be seen is in the park,
near where Bird removed the Brontosaur trail.*

Brontosaur track just below the Park Ledge.

Man-like trail on the Park Ledge. These prints are marked with faint yellow paint. Rangers used to show them, but no longer.

Just below the edge of the Park Ledge are two large Brontosaur tracks.

to the air and to moving water for many years and are rapidly eroding.

But more importantly, on the ledge above the brontosaur tracks are human-like tracks, over a dozen of them of various sizes. Several are in stride, others are in a standing position, and some are found just at random. In years past the park rangers had marked some of these with yellow paint and showed them to those who asked. Now, of course, the present-day rangers claim to have no knowledge of the existence of the man-like prints nor of the showings in previous years. However, the faded yellow paint remains.

This ledge may be reached by crossing the river on a stepping stone foot bridge. Thousands of visitors walk all over the ledge each year, and the prints have been nearly worn away. Comparison of photos in the late sixties with more recent ones shows the effect of the wear.

Also on the ledge are two very unusual tracks that look more bear-like than anything else. They are wide with five claw-like marks. The two prints are at opposite ends of the ledge.

The fossil layer at the downstream end of the ledge contains a good number of fossil clams, all tightly shut. Just downstream shallow ruts in the river bottom lessen in depth and finally disappear. In their places remain recent joints or cracks in the rock.

Point 22 (Overlook)

The river bottom is rough and broken between the park ledge, around the bend in the river, and in the second most popular visitor attraction, an overlook which affords a view of clear tyrannosaur tracks crossing the river at right angles. These are usually kept clean and are visible through the water. About 100 feet downstream are two brontosaur tracks that are seldom seen.

A fossil layer, exposed at the downstream end of the Park Ledge contains many fossil clams and gastropods.

A well-preserved gastropod found in the fossil layer overlying the main footprint layer. Name: Tylostoma travisensis.

Far below is a clear set of dinosaur prints crossing the Paluxy. They can be seen from the park road overlook above. Note the ruts crossing the trail.

At point 23, large impressions can be seen which are roughly in stride and generally shaped like a large human foot.

Point 23

Another 150 yards or so downstream are some good dinosaur prints on a ledge on the right side of the river. There are several poorly formed man-like prints as well, roughly in sequence, but lacking any real detail.

Burdick site. Large moccasin-like tracks heading shoreward led to the excavation of the bank. An additional track was found. (c) *FFC.*

Point 24 (Burdick Site) — See Appendix

It is very difficult to reach the river from above in this vicinity. The cliff at the overlook extends around the bend and is rather hard to climb, up or down. Near the camping area several paths have been graded and access is possible.

Near a five-foot exposure of the fossil layer, several large foot-shaped holes can be seen in the river, some in a vague "stride." Dr. Burdick noted them years ago, and choosing the most likely prospect, he and the Taylor crew dug back into the bank and found a trail of "moccasin" tracks. The prints are quite large and punch all the way through the print layer into the clay layer below.

Point 25 (Denio Branch)

Throughout the downstream end of the park as the river curves back around and heads south, no prints of any sort have been found until Denio Branch is reached. Here are several trails of well defined dinosaur tracks heading in all directions. It seems to have been a place of confusion or loitering. This would be a good place to sandbag.

Point 26

The water in this area is usually rather deep and slow moving. When the river makes a thirty-degree turn to the right, the limestone marker bed, so prominent and helpful on the other side of the park, reappears. The print layer is covered by a thick layer of river cobbles.

Point 27 (Third Crossing)

There is a nice swimming hole just off the old low water bridge, visible from the newer, elevated bridge.

Point 28 (Shakey Springs) — See Appendix

Just upstream from the place where the small Lake Reed empties into the Paluxy, the ground is of unique consistency and saturated with water. Jumping up and down causes trees and fence posts to vibrate some distance away.

More pertinent to our discussion, however, are numerous trails of a three-toed dinosaur unlike most in the area. This author is unaware of any formal de-

Shakey Springs. Many varied prints, including some dinosaur prints which can be mistaken for human prints. The fossil layer here is loaded with clams.

scription of the particular dinosaur which made these prints, but they play an important role in this study.

The prints are definitely elongated, much like human prints. But on the front of each print are three pencil-thin appendages, from 4" - 6" long, not at all like the toes on most dinosaur prints. Perhaps they are claw marks, but then, again, no dinosaur known to this author had such a foot. The trails are of different sizes and strides, and unless a careful investigator discovers the marks, the prints and trails can be misunderstood. Once these prints were understood, it was obvious that the McFall trail of eroded prints had a similar origin and were not made by human feet.

The rock here is covered with a rather spongy weathered surface, and it might be valuable to clean it off to see if the prints are more definitive at depth. But there are clear prints of the more common dinosaur and even some prints which look rather man-like. This area needs further study.

The four-foot rubble-fossil layer which here lies under the marker bed contains the highest percentage of clam fossils of any area along the Paluxy. Some are marvelously well preserved, with even the clam shell and its coloring visible.

Point 29 (Mack Farm) — See Appendix

In the summer of 1976, an ICR-sponsored group of volunteer workers had intended to investigate the bottom of a deep pool near the Robert Mack farm just upstream from the second crossing, but due to local flooding they accomplished little. The area was studied in 1978 when the river and pool completely dried up.

Eight different types of dinosaurs are represented here. University geology departments frequently bring

Upstream of the 2nd crossing, near the Mack farm, is an area with many well-preserved dinosaur prints. Here Dr. Ed Blick is sweeping them clean.

field trips to this location. Baylor University studies have been the most extensive, but of course, the idea of man prints is ridiculed. Numerous elongated markings are visible and Dougherty has for years claimed they are human. Many disagree, including this author, feeling instead that the markings are either "tail drags" or eroded joints, as described earlier.

The dinosaur prints are preserved in exquisite detail. Since the conditions are so favorable, the area should be studied carefully. Caution is urged, however, since the top of the print layer is somewhat soft, but in most places not extensively eroded, due to the normal depth of water. Less than 100 feet downstream from the area of main interest, dinosaur prints are clearly seen in two different layers.

Point 30

Nearing the second crossing, a team of investigators discovered a carbonized stick imbedded in the upper surface of the print layer. It was about 8' long and straight. It seemed to have been burning as it fell into the once soft sediments. Samples were sent to the UCLA carbon-14 dating laboratory, which placed the death of the plant at $12,800 \pm 200$ years ago. In 1969 and 1971, Stanley Taylor found carbonized material in the limestone, with dating results varying from 38,000 years to 900 years! Fred Beierle had also found carbonized leaves in his 1976 excavation; in fact, geologic literature describing the stratigraphy calls attention to the preservation of such material in the Glen Rose Limestone, but since the formation is far too "old" for carbon-14 measurements to be meaningful, no prior efforts were made to determine its age.

Point 31 (Second Crossing)

To get to the second crossing by car, turn south off

Unusual markings at the 4th crossing. When the river is dry, almost any shape can be found. Caution is absolutely necessary when studying footprints.

Small, well-preserved dinosaur print near the Mack farm.

of Highway 205 at the "sucker-rod" fence (white drilling pipe). There is a good place to park in the middle of the shallow wide river.

Point 32

No prints are found for about one-half mile downstream from the second crossing. The print layer does form the river bottom, however, for the so-called "tail drags" gnarl the river.

Point 33 (West of Gauging Station)

Some very good dinosaur prints rest in two layers about 8" apart, about one-quarter mile upstream from the water gauging station. The upper layer has less distinct prints and could easily be tipped over exposing the more distinct layer below.

Point 34 (First Crossing)

U.S. Highway 67 crosses the river at this point.

Point 35 (Glen Rose) — See Appendix

Between the bridges in Glen Rose, the water is usually quite deep and rather polluted. The print layer is covered by more than a foot of loose rock, mud, and trash. No prints can be seen. Near the bridge in Glen Rose are several features worth mentioning. Linear joints on both sides of the bridge can, under certain circumstances, look like trails of man tracks and have been so reported on occasion.

The controversial prints owned by Al Berry in New Mexico, seen by Roland Bird, and purchased by Bob Gentry in recent years are considered by most to be fake. Berry, however, in his affidavit, claimed to have hired a jack hammer operator, working on the construction of the small dam, to remove them from the river at this point. It might be worthwhile to clean off

Just behind the Snyder Sanitorium is a small dam, shown here when the river was dry. Several of the prints in Columbia Union College were reportedly found here.

the river bottom behind the small dam to see if other prints remain or perhaps holes in the riverbed might provide a clue. Just below the dam are three rather nondescript markings in a very rough rock that Dougherty claims are human prints in stride. These are not clear enough to be certain, however.

Decades ago Glen Rose was a resort area of sorts, claiming healing powers for the local mineral-laden water. The once popular Snyder Sanatorium, on the north of the river at this point, once inspired the writing of a popular Elvis Presley song when the huge oak tree on the riverbank became immortalized as "The Singing Tree."

Downstream from Glen Rose the ruts in the river bed (above), which normally parallel the river flow, are in two intersecting systems, one following the river and the other following the river at a previous time.

Here the joints (left) grade laterally into a fine crack near the bank, establishing their origin.

Point 36 (Big Rock City Park)

Downstream from the Bridge in Glen Rose, where the river bends to the south, big boulders lie strewn about. In fact, the area is called Big Rocks City Park. The boulders are the eroded remains of the massive Thorp Spring carbonate member prominent in the park. Even though the area is frequently visited, it is a haven for rattlesnakes.

Point 37

As the river makes a horseshoe turn back to the north, the joints in the print layer are unique. In all other areas the joints (or tail drags) follow the river, but here they intersect the bank on both sides of the horseshoe, evidently following a previous river channel. Another series of joints intersects the main series at about a thirty-degree angle and reflects the change in river location.

These secondary joints forced the conclusion that at least some of the ruts in the river are not tail drags, as previously thought. Here the deep ruts grade laterally into sharp, thin fractures nearer the shore.

This listing of major trails and print sites includes all sites of interest known to this investigator. Undoubtedly other prints and points of interest have been and will be discovered. It is hoped that this mapping system will be used to document them. For example, by proportioning the distance between points 15 and 16, a print could be located at point 15.6.

There are some other nearby sites. Slim Adams remembers seeing a trail of five moccasin prints in Rock Creek south of town. They were so clear that a leather thong or flap of some kind could be seen in every other print. A series of large moccasin-like tracks have also been found on Cross Branch, also south of Glen Rose.

More recently, while excavating a pond on his property, Adams found dozens of other prints. The prints were not in rock, but in mud. When he tipped over a layer of limestone (presumably the marker bed) the prints were in the soft clay layer below. Molds of the prints remained in the bottom of the hard overlying layer. He did not take the time to search for human prints, but he did save the mold of a print that appears to be human. Since a print in unconsolidated clay would disappear in a short time, this discovery is another of the evidences for rapid deposition of sediments. There is no possibility that the sediments are due to a slow transgression of the sea.

Other sets of dinosaur tracks have been found on some of the nearby tributaries of the Paluxy, or so the locals say, but these have not been adequately studied. Dinosaur prints have also been found on the Leon

The only place clear prints are not in or near the river bottom. Here about 10 dinosaur and several man-like prints can be seen (Point 5).

West property on the Brazos River near where Highway 67 crosses the Brazos and on the Sealy Lease SE, along Squaw Creek, a Brazos Tributary.

Two dinosaur trails were found in May, 1975, during excavation for the Commanche Peak nuclear power plant five miles north of Glen Rose. The plant location is near Squaw Creek.

SUMMARY

Point	Description	Comments
1	Ford west of cemetery	Westerly end of investigation.
2	Lanham Mill cemetery	
3	Road on Rock Shelf	Marker bed forms part of the road.
4	McFall Site	Fifteen eroded dinosaur tracks which some have called human. Print four is missing. Prints = 18" long with 54" stride. Cross two other dinosaur trails.
5	Prints on Ledge	About five feet above water level. Ten dinosaur tracks and six man-like tracks. Stratigraphy uncertain.
6	Prints Underwater	Several eroded man-like trails and prints can be seen underwater.
7	Moss 1908 Prints	Site of trail washed away in 1918. Series of four eroded man-like prints nearby.
8	Old Lanham Mill	Removed man and dinosaur prints from same spot. Tracks raised.
9	Taylor Site	Site of most of Taylor's and

Turnage's work. Excavated for *Footprints in Stone* movie and by others more recently. Here are four man trails and two dinosaur trails.

10 Long Dinosaur Trail
According to Turnage, well over one hundred dinosaur tracks in sequence, a world's record. An excellent place to study.

11 Turnage man-like tracks
Turnage abandoned this trail after investigation, although the prints are better than some. The debris covered shelf should be opened up.

12 Dougherty Site
Several man-like trails and good dinosaur prints. The best print found in recent years was discovered here. Area should be expanded along with Point 11.

13 Fourth Crossing
Closed to public travel.

14 Dinosaur Cast
Anomalous cast of dinosaur track.

15 Noticeable change in dip

16 Marker bed pinches out
Resistant limestone bed thins and is replaced by a rubble layer and then by a fossil layer.

17 Blue Hole
Good dinosaur prints, some penetrating through to layer below. Good place to swim.

18 Oppossum Branch
A few dinosaur prints found

		above the fossil layer.
19	Bird Excavation	Roland Bird removed his series of dinosaur tracks from here. Local residents recall a series of man-like tracks.
20	Field's Brontosaur trails	Three brontosaur trails—largest is 85' long, containing 21 tracks.
21	Park Ledge	Main tourist site. Good brontosaurus prints and several human prints in second layer. Many fossils here.
22	Overlook	Tourist site. See two striking dinosaur trails from above.
23	Dinosaur Prints	Also several random man-like prints. Need more study here.
24	Burdick's Trail	Three large moccasin tracks which penetrate the layer into the mud below.
25	Denio Branch	Many well-preserved dinosaur prints. Good area to study.
26	Marker bed reappears	The marker bed here overlies but does not completely replace the fossil and rubble layer as before.
27	Third Crossing	Old abandoned low water bridge replaced by elevated one. Swimming hole.
28	Shakey Springs	Important dinosaur trails here. Many fossils, spongy ground, Lake Reed drains here.

29	Mack Farm	Site of 1976 ICR and 1978 Beierle-Fields investigations. No certain human prints, but eight varieties of distinct dinosaur prints.
30	Carbonized Stick	Found imbedded in print layer.
31	Second Crossing	
32	"Tail drags"	
33	w/o Gauging Station	Excellent dinosaur prints in two layers. No man prints seen, but area should be studied.
34	First Crossing	U.S. Highway 67.
35	Bridge in Glen Rose	Near the dam is reported to be source of Berry tracks.
36	Big Rocks City Park	
37	Intersecting Joints	

There is no doubt that the print-bearing layers are part of the regional stratigraphy. The same general column dominates throughout the area of study and correlated with the column at the nuclear plant site. The Glen Rose Member extends to the Southeast all the way into the Gulf of Mexico, although buried deeply.

Tracks are found in more than one layer in the same location at Points 9, 14, 21, 29, and 33, and, according to unpublished reports, at the nuclear plant site.

Several areas require more investigation and could possibly yield valuable information. Point 10 could be sandbagged to expose the long dinosaur trail, but since the known human trails come from that direction, it is reasonable to expect to find others. Points 11 and 12 both have possible man tracks and removal of the debris pile could be fruitful. Points 7, 25, and 28 could be studied with a minimum of equipment and are very important areas. Study requires only owner's permission since they are not inside the park. Point 33 looks interesting, but it would require the removal of a rock layer, which under the present regulations is not possible.

Chapter 11

Reconstructing Noah's Flood

In previous chapters it has been shown that the layer of rock which contains the prints must have been laid down rapidly, and that it could not have been the bottom of a lagoon or a beach deposit. The material when deposited must have had a cementing agent or stabilizer that quickly hardened the rock sufficiently to keep the prints from being washed away.

The presence and types of fossils preserved in the rock and the layers above and below also speak of rapid burial and lithification. The layer immediately above the print layer contains literally millions of fossil clams, all tightly closed in their living position. These and other fossils in the layer were not buried after death, but were buried alive.

The presence of carbonized wood and plant material, which is one of the diagnostic features of the Glen Rose Limestone, also speaks eloquently of rapid burial. What is a long stick or large plank doing at the bottom of a lagoon or tidal zone, unless it is trapped there by flood water deposition of massive amounts of sedimentary material? The fact that the Glen Rose

Limestone covers half of Texas and Mexico and much of the Gulf of Mexico with a thickness of hundreds of feet shows that this deposition could not have been merely a local phenomenon.

To be permanently preserved, the footprints, rain markings, and ripple marks, once made in the hardening sediments, would need an effective covering. In this case, the prints must have been filled in by a layer of clay, washed in soon after they were made, or else they would have eroded. In other words, each layer must not have been only deposited rapidly, but there could have been no long time gaps between the deposition of successive layers.

Since surface markings exist throughout the geologic column, it can be shown that unless an erosional sequence took place between the deposition of two layers, they must have been laid down in rapid succession. But even erosional episodes would not preclude the indication of continuous sedimentation, since when traced laterally, all unconformities (erosional surfaces) are found to disappear and each layer grades conformably into the next higher layer, showing that erosion was only a local (although perhaps extensive) effect. The fact that there are no worldwide unconformities is evidence that the deposition process always continued somewhere in the world. Therefore, the major part of the entire geologic column can easily be interpreted in light of continued deposition associated with a major water catastrophe.

The obvious testimony of Scripture yields the same conclusion. The Bible speaks of a year-long water catastrophe that covered the highest mountains. Any such cataclysm would clearly have been geologically significant and capable of the formation of the geologic column.

The fact that human and dinosaur prints are found

together supports such a reconstruction. There is no way to interpret this evidence within the standard evolutionary-uniformitarian model. Without a doubt the catastrophe model fits the data much better than does the uniformitarian model.

Unfortunately, the catastrophe model is not without its own problems, and some of the data are hard to incorporate. This is due partly to the fact that catastrophism is a relatively new conceptual framework for science, and also to the fact that very few investigators with geologic knowledge have tried to interpret specific geologic data from this perspective.

Perhaps the main problem in this interpretation of the Glen Rose area lies underground. A cross section of Texas showing the subsurface reveals that about 8,500 feet of water-borne Paleozoic and Mesozoic sediments directly underlie the Paluxy River. If these sediments are to be understood as having been deposited during the flood of Noah, how could any living thing, man or dinosaur, witness such massive deposition at the beginning stages of the flood and still be alive to leave their footprints on top? Just to the east, the strata dip away and plunge into the Gulf Coast Basin where similar sequences of rock are 50,000 feet thick in places. It seems unreasonable that man could have postponed annihilation for so long. And even if animals and men were still alive, how could they have made their footprints in the midst of such turmoil?

Some have reasoned that the man prints may have been made during the closing years of the Ice Age as huge volumes of melt water once again deposited sediments. Certainly man was in North America by the time of the Ice Age, for human fossils are found in glacial deposits.

However, these regionally extensive deposits are definitely of marine origin, not glacial, as indicated by both the types of rocks and fossils. To the east, the beds are conformable and thick and are undoubtedly flood deposits. The layers above and below, all laid down in rapid succession, are likewise of marine origin. These rocks were certainly laid down during the flood of Noah's day, not during the Ice Age following.

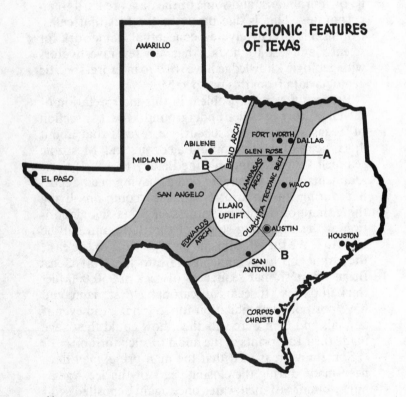

11-a

Tectonic features of Texas, showing Llano Uplift as a possible place of safety during the early stages of the flood. The shaded area is where the Glen Rose limestone might be on the surface. (Redrawn from the A.A.P.G. Geologic Highway map of Texas.)

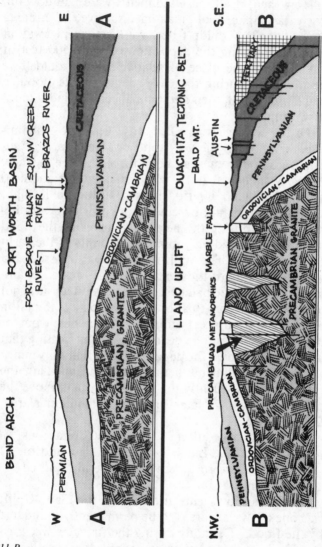

11-B

Cross sections of Texas through the Glen Rose area (A-A) and through the Llano Uplife (B-B), as located on the previous map. (Redrawn from the A.A.P.G. Geologic Highway map of Texas.)

How then, if all these sediments were laid down in one catastrophe, could man have survived in this area for so long? Wouldn't he have been swept away at some time during the deposition of the 8,500 feet of material? Some place of relative safety would have been needed during the early stages of the flood, a place where both men and animals could find temporary refuge.

To the southwest of Glen Rose lies a possible answer. Almost in the very center of Texas a Precambrian granitic dome has been forced to the surface. A nearly circular feature, with a diameter of about 60 miles, the Llano Uplift forms a stratigraphic high. This highly resistant basement rock was evidently being uplifted during the beginning stages of the flood because it received only minimal amounts of the earliest sediments. The uplift was probably associated with the sinking of the nearby Gulf of Mexico, maintaining an isostatic balance. The strata on all sides not only dip away from this feature, due to a combination of uplift and adjacent subsidence, but pinch out or become thinner as they near the uplift, indicating that uplift accompanied the deposition and that only minor amounts of sediments actually were trapped on the rising dome. Evidently the uplift projected above the rising flood waters later than the surrounding area. Davis claims:

> During deposition of lowermost Cretaceous sediments, the Llano Uplift was an island of Pre-Mesozoic rocks covering several hundred square miles.[1]

The conclusion seems justified that the Llano Uplift was one of the last areas to be permanently inundated by the flood. Certainly during the first few weeks of the flood, as torrential rains poured down, as waters rose, as the earth shifted, and as areas flooded, men and the more mobile animals would have sought the highest ground for safety (which in this region would have been this great rock mass). Animals of various sorts, friends and former enemies alike, would have rushed about in near panic looking for permanent safety. Perhaps the men built rafts in a futile effort to save themselves.

A temporary lowering of the water level, perhaps due to rapid sinking of the adjacent Gulf, nearby faulting, tsunamis in other areas of the world, or any of a number of possible causes would have exposed some of the recently deposited sediments. In their frantic search for safety, many animals left the uplift only to later find that the waters returned, even higher than before. A map of the numerous dinosaur track locations in the Glen Rose limestone in Texas indicates that the dinosaurs plodded off in all directions, leaving their footprints in the fresh sediments as they went. In fact, the location of the tracks in the Glen Rose Limestone accurately outlines the fringes of the Llano Uplife itself. [2]

The rim of the subsiding Gulf of Mexico runs north from the Uplift into Oklahoma. At the time the Glen Rose Limestone was being deposited, much of western Texas was completely flooded and the sinking of the water level to the east exposed this northward trending arch. No doubt some of the fleeing animals and men followed this natural causeway in their frantic effort to escape destruction. Only the Upper Cretaceous beds seem to be continuous on both sides of the arch, but these beds were to come later.

The present-day town of Glen Rose, nearly the farthest north of the known footprint locations, lies only 25 miles east of the high point of the Bend Arch on line with the extension of the Lampasas Arch. Furthermore, it is 50 miles west of the Ouachita Tectonic Belt

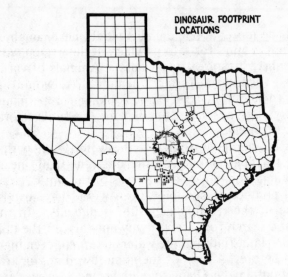

DINOSAUR FOOTPRINT
LOCATIONS

Dinosaur footprints have been found in numerous places in the Glen Rose Limestone, all surrounding the Llano Uplift, implying that the Uplift was one of the last places to be covered by the rising flood waters. (See the following list.) (Modified from Perkins.)

1. *Squaw Creek and Nuclear Plant Site, Somervell County.*
2. *Paluxy River and Brazos River near Glen Rose, Somervell County.*
3. *Bosque River near Iredell, Bosque County.*
4. *Lake Eanes, Comanche County.*
5. *Cowhouse Creek, near Indian Gap, Hamilton County.*
6. *Cottonwood Creek, Hamilton County.*
7. *South San Gabriel River, Williamson County.*
8. *Colorado River, 15 miles N/O Austin, Travis County.*
9. *Perdenales River, Perdenales Falls State Park, Blanco County.*
10. *Blanco River, 3 miles W/O Blanco, Blanco County.*
11. *Garner Ranch, Kimble County.*
12. *Guadalupe River near Hunt, Kerr County.*
13. *Hondo Creek, 3 miles N/O Tarpley, Bandera County.*
14. *Mayan Ranch, Bandera County.*
15. *Hondo Creek, 2 miles S/O Tarpley, Bandera County.*
16. *Middle Verde River, near Tarpley, Bandera County.*
17. *Davenport Ranch, Medina County.*
18. *Hondo Creek, 13 miles NW/O Hondo, Medina County.*
19. *Sabinal River, 4 miles S/O Utopia, Uvalde County.*
20. *Live Oak Creek, near West Nueces River, Kinney County.*

which was also being uplifted, although more slowly than the Llano Uplift. Glen Rose is only 100 miles or so from the Uplift itself.

It is not at all inconceivable that a few hardy souls could have survived the early onslaughts of the flood as the water rose. It is also quite possible that conditions allowed their migration to areas surrounding the Uplift, including Glen Rose, to leave their footprints in the mud before being finally overwhelmed by the returning waters. Even though these speculations are not to be considered as established fact, they are consistent with all geologic facts that have come to this author's attention. The argument that the flood model is unbelievable because land animals could not have survived 8,500 feet of deposition is found to be insufficient.

References for Chapter 11

1. Davis, Keith W., "Stratigraphy and Depositional Environments of the Glen Rose Formation, North-Central Texas," *Baylor Geological Society Bulletin,* No. 26, 1974, p. 9.
2. Perkins, B.F., Ed., "Dinosaur Valley State Park" in *Trace Fossils, a Field Guide to Selected Localities in Pennsylvanian, Permian, Cretaceous, and Tertiary Rocks of Texas,* Baton Rouge: Louisiana State University, misc. publ., 71-1, 1971, p. 56-59.

Chapter 12

Continuing Research

Early in May, 1979, a major flood roared down the Paluxy. Water depths, which are normally less than three feet, were up to thirty feet. Vast damage was done to nearby farms, roads, and structures. Trees were uprooted and scattered about. When it retreated the water left a layer of slippery mud covering everything in sight. After it was over, witnesses spoke in awe of the frightening noise of the smashing together of boulders and rock slabs as they tumbled along.

Back in 1908, as you recall, a similar flood ripped through the area, exposing rock ledges for the first time—ledges which contained footprints of certain animals, including humans and dinosaurs. On other occasions, equally tragic floods have either exposed or removed vital rock layers on which prints were visible. No doubt future storms will follow, and new areas of interest will be opened, while known areas will be destroyed.

Who knows? It may be that one such storm will expose a set of footprints as good as the one Charlie Moss saw as a youngster. Or perhaps the one print right next to the rock ledge at the Dougherty site may have others in the trail which would be visible if a por-

At times the Paluxy rages out of control, some 25' higher than normal water levels. In this picture the water is about 3' higher than normal.

tion of the ledge broke off. Perhaps nothing more will ever be found, but then again perhaps the perfect trail, with tracks of great detail which would constitute evidence that no one with an open mind could refute, will someday be found.

The Institute for Creation Research (and in particular this author) maintains an active interest. Previously ICR had sponsored some of Burdick's and Turnage's work and in 1976 sponsored a large group of volunteer workers. In 1977 a complete survey of the area was undertaken, while in 1978 final documentation of certain trails took place. In 1979, on-location filming of interviews prepared the way for presentation of the information to a new international viewing audience.

Mr. Fred Beierle's interest and involvement resulted in an effort in 1976, partially sponsored by the Bible-

Science Association, to dig down to the print layer from the property adjacent to the Taylor site, using a rented backhoe. The following year he reexposed the Taylor site to gain a better perspective on future excavation sites. In 1978, while the river was dry, he searched for new evidence, discovering what is now called the Beierle Trail. Beierle's interesting book, *Man, Dinosaur, and History,* can be ordered from the Bible-Science Association, P. O. Box 6131, Minneapolis, Minnesota 55406.

Groups from the Ozark Bible College of Joplin, Missouri, led by Professor Wilbur Fields, joined with Beierle on occasion and at other times worked separately. In 1977 and 1978, several of the most important trails were surveyed and documented, and some of Fields' work is included in the Appendix of this book. Following both 1977 and 1978 investigation, Fields and crew published preliminary reports. These well-illustrated and informative monographs can be obtained from Ozark Bible College, 1111 North Main Street, Joplin, Missouri 64801.

The former president of the Missouri Association for Creation Science, Mr. Rex Hess, recruited many of the volunteer workers for the 1977-1978 efforts, and the Association has consistently maintained interest and involvement in the project.

In nearby Dallas, Professor John Voss of the Dallas Bible College recently began to take an even more active role in the study of the Paluxy; his classes have been treated to field trips and work weekends. Much of the progress of recent years resulted from labors of the dedicated D.B.C. students.

Dr. Cecil Dougherty recently retired from his practice and moved away from Glen Rose. However, his long involvement in the footprint search draws him back. His enjoyable booklet, *Valley of the Giants,* can be obtained from the Somervell County Museum, Glen Rose, Texas 76043.

Mr. Walter DiPietro of Fort Worth has made numerous trips to the Paluxy since his involvement with ICR's 1976 expedition. In 1978, he cleaned off several of the major trails (a fact for which later groups were thankful) and investigated a report that human prints existed near Iredell, Texas, as well.

Other individuals and organizations, whose contributions have not been insignificant, could be listed, but the list would be long, and many are mentioned elsewhere in this book. The point to be made is that the continuance of the project is assured. By keeping in touch with ICR and the other groups, the reader will be made aware of future efforts, as well as opportunities to join them.

Certainly this book with its maps and photos will allow even the casual visitor to enjoy and understand the Paluxy more fully. It may even be the catalyst to encourage further research, in search of more convincing evidence.

However, unless flood waters expose some new areas, it is not likely that important new trails will be found. Since the establishment of the state park, no excavation is allowed. Even outside the park boundaries, no permanent alterations are permissible and even the building of a sandbag dam requires permits from the state.

The park has purchased much of the land containing the best tracks, but it does not yet have it all. Approaches have been made at various times to owners of the land on either side of the Taylor site to consider selling it to a creationist organization, with the thought of sponsoring a year-round "dig" on private property and the additional dream of building a creation museum on the site. The cost of the proposed project has slowed serious consideration, but sporadic communication maintains hope. Interested individuals are invited to discuss the potential with this author or several of the other workers.

It must be stressed that while success cannot be guaranteed to any future project, the evidence already available should be sufficient to convince all but the most skeptical. If one allows the whole body of data to speak for itself, without attempting to harmonize it with preconceived ideas, the conclusion that man and dinosaur walked together at the same time and place— and that both perished in a watery cataclysm—seems inevitable.

Appendix

Appendix

Detailed Descriptions of the Major Human Trails

The locations of all known human trails, as well as the major dinosaur trails and geologic landmarks, have been described in Chapter 10, so that interested persons can find them. In this appendix is given a detailed description of each human trail, so that as erosion takes it toll on the appearance of the prints (as it has already done on many of the prints), at least there will be a permanent record. This summary attempts to document both all known human trails, as well as those that have been called "human" by some investigators.

Some of the trails have been surveyed and carefully mapped; others remain only in the memory of those fortunate enough to have seen them. The writer has been involved in several of the mapping efforts, but will also rely heavily on work done by other investigators.

For the sake of clarity and continuity, this listing will follow the framework set up in Chapter 10, starting at the most upstream of the human or human-like trails, describing it, and proceeding downstream, referencing them to the location numbers and names. It is important to have a good grasp of the nature of the prints and trails before attempting to use or extend the data.

Point 3. Series of four indistinct markings on the marker bed.
Photo by Dougherty

Point 3 (Highway 205)

Where the marker bed becomes the road for a while,

Dr. Dougherty has found some very indistinct markings in the marker bed which he has tentatively labeled as "human." While it is true that the four "prints" in sequence bear some resemblance to human trails, it should be recognized that the marker bed here is extremely uneven, and almost any shape marking is possible. It should also be noted that there are no clear prints in the marker bed anywhere in the Paluxy River valley; therefore, these prints are questionable. This author has only seen pictures of them, but remains unconvinced.

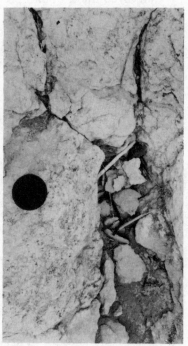

McFall Trail. Eroded, V-shaped, elongated dinosaur prints. Have been mistaken for human prints.

Photo by Dougherty

Several of the prints at the McFall site have heel spur marks in addition to three toe marks. They should not be considered human.

Point 4 (McFall Site)

The series of 14 prints on the south bank of the river had been thought by some to be human tracks, but three marks on the upstream end of several of the tracks (such as seen on the Shakey Springs prints) rule out this interpretation. Taylor and crew had removed the overlying ledge with a tractor, air hammer, jacks and pry bars, and had exposed 17 elongated prints in stride. This trail is crossed by two more obvious but eroded dinosaur trails. Wilbur Fields and company surveyed the trail and provided much of the following data.

Number of prints visible: 14 (1 missing, 2 covered)

Average Length:	21"
Average Width:	4" - 6"
Stride:	45"
Appearance:	V-shaped and eroded
Direction of travel:	S 60° E, but somewhat meandering.

The destructive flood in the spring of 1979 broke off two large chunks of the layer which hosted the prints, and now only about half of the prints remain.

Point 5 (Elevated Print Layer)

In one of the few places where prints are out of the water (here about six feet above the river bottom) are several large man-like tracks. Taylor uncovered the lateral extension at this trail and writes in a "special Report"[1]:

> Several large man-like tracks had been noted here where the surface rock had been eroded back. They ran parallel to the river and then curved directly away from it. Operating from the river, the scoop operator was able to reach the top operating ledge and lift back several

large slabs. As a result, we uncovered three previously unexposed man-like tracks. It was obvious that the footprints had been made in deep mud and the mud had partially run together as the foot had been withdrawn.

Mr. McFall also shows a few single man-like impressions in the overlying marker bed, but these do not appear to be true prints.

In the middle of the river at this point Taylor found several markings which had faint toe impressions, but was unable to study them carefully at the time, and subsequent studies have not been made.

Point 6 (Ware Prints)

James Ware, who had worked with Turnage in 1971, writes about the sandbagging and study of several trails exposed at low water levels on the Kerr side of the river:[2]

> We found a possibility of five or six new trails, all eroded by the stream. These did appear to be human, both as to stride and size, with elongated narrow tracks. It also appeared that some trails overlapped, with one of the trails branching into a Y shape. We concluded that too many people making tracks simultaneously, plus the erosional factor made this site interesting, but not as good due to the indistinct toes, etc. The trails are there, but good, well defined footprints are not.

Point 7 (Moss Prints)

Charlie Moss' notarized record is reproduced in Chapter 2. He also provided the following additional information in a taped interview with Dr. George Westcott. The tracks were pointing east and were "shaped in detail with clear heel marks, prominent arches, and all five toes showing. Mud had come up between all the toes with the exception of the fourth and fifth on each foot, which seemed to be closer together than the other toes. They, however, made separate and distinct indentations. The most impressive thing was not the long stride, but the unusual length of the tracks."[3]

Unfortunately, the prints were destroyed by a flood in 1918, and no pictures were taken before their destruction.

Almost directly across the river, exactly 85 feet upstream from the circular hole at Point 8, is another series of man-like tracks. According to Westcott, they lie "nine feet out from a rocky ledge that rises abruptly out of the water. Four tracks make up the series and . . . all point westward. A left, right, and a left one in sequence, then four tracks are missing. The final track is 27 feet from the first track and represents the right foot. The average stride is 46 inches and the lateral separation is 6 inches. The individual tracks are about 13 inches long. They lack detail, but are long and narrow. The toe and heel are easily differentiated."[4]

Point 8 (Old Lanham Mill)

The hole near the fence crossing the river behind the McFall home measures 50" x 60". Jim Ryals claims to have removed a slab here containing both a human and a dinosaur track. Four raised three-toed dinosaur tracks are visible, while the moccasin tracks are usually under the debris on the shoreline, but all are poorly defined.

Point 9 (Taylor Site)

About halfway between the McFall home and the well-known Taylor site, Jacob McFall and two of his

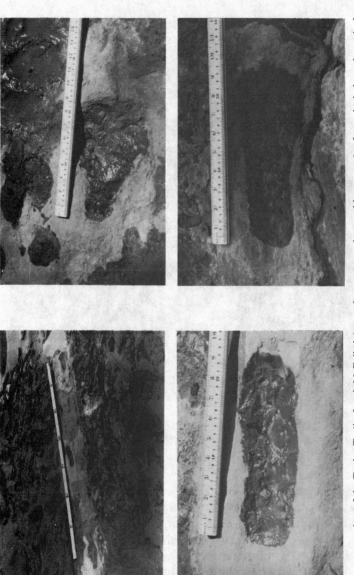

The upper portion of the Taylor Trail. Jacob McFall claims to have removed a good human print from the hole at the end of the measuring stick in the photo in the upper left. The three prints shown lead up to the hole, with the toes in the final track (lower right) having been cut off in removal. © FFC photos by P. Taylor.

The lower portion of the Taylor Trail. The hole in the lower left is an exploratory hole. Three of the prints very nearly step on dinosaur track. Note coiled cloth tape measure for size.

friends, the Wilson brothers, had cut a good human print out of the rock. Taylor relocated this hole and three human tracks leading up to it.

The track immediately behind the "cut out" showed an impression of the ball of the foot, instep, and heel, although the toes were missing as Jacob had said (removed when chiseling

out the better track). The track behind this
showed the general shape of a human foot with
an instep. Both were about 9½ inches in
length. The third imprint showed only the impression that would have been made by the ball
of the foot with no clear toe impressions. Beyond this the stratum dipped leaving no impressions.[5]

Much of the work in succeeding years had been carried out at the lower end of the Taylor site where four
or possibly five clear human trails have been found.
They are known as (as seen on the accompanying map)
the Taylor Trail, the Turnage Trail, the Giant Run,
the Ryals Trail, and the Beierle Trail.

Taylor Trail

Fields established an effective numbering system for
this trail. As the area within the impoundment was
pumped out, the first print in the series to appear
above the water was labeled number +1. Those succeeding it were labeled +2, +3, etc., and those preceding it were labeled -1, -2, -3, etc. The label H-1
given this trail by Turnage reflects the first human (H)
trail studied at this site. The prints are, as of this writing, much less distinct than in 1970, but the trail is
impressive. The following tabulation is modified from
Fields' work,[6] with dimensions as measured in 1970 by
Films for Christ given in parenthesis adjacent to the
corresponding dimensions as measured by Fields in
1977. The extensive erosion has altered the prints and
many important features—such as toe prints—have
been completely destroyed.

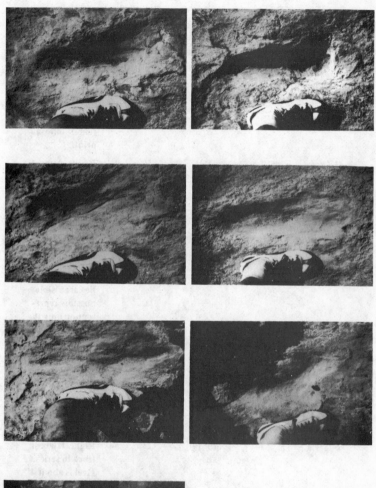

*Taylor Trail. Previous page: Upper left
H-1;-7, through H-1;-2 lower right.
This page: Upper left H-1;-1, through
H-1;+6.*

Number	Width at toe	Length	Depth at ball	Stride to next Print	Comments
H-1,(-7)	-	-	-	50"	A probe hole drilled searching for print -7
H-1, -6	5"	16"	1"	20"	Right
H-1, -5	5"	16"	1"	80"	Left. Very near rear of dinosaur print.
H-1, -4	5"	15"	1"	91"	Right. Almost touching side of dinosaur print.
H-1, -3b	-	-	-		Very likely two prints with small strides are missing between print -4 and -3. Two small irregularities are visible possibly representing only the ball and toe areas of each foot.
H-1, -3c	-	-	-		
H-1, -3	6"	15"	1"	52"	Left (Turnage numbering system H-1-1)
H-1, -2	6½"	16"	2"	56"	Right
H-1, -1	6"	15"	2"	54"	Left
H-1, +1	5½"(4)	15"(9)	2"	54"	Right. Highest track in series. Heel is about 4" deep. Very near 2nd dinosaur trail.
H-1, +2	6½"(4)	16"(12)	2"	49"	Left
H-1, +3	5½"(4)	18"(13-16)	½"	54"	Right—heel slid.
H-1, +4	5½"(3½)	18"(12-16)	1¼"	44"	Left—indistinct 5 splash marks.

H-1, +5	5"(4)	16"(12)	1½"	49"	Right—splash mark.
H-1, +6	5"(4)	11"(9)	1"		Left—Concretions mark toe area.
H-1, +7 to +21					The remainder of this series was not exposed when the above survey was carried out.

Taylor, when bulldozing the area during the filming of the movie *Footprints in Stone,* was able to expose the extension of this trail which has not been exposed since. He counted 23 tracks in the trail, although in 1970 the first 4 tracks of the Turnage Trail were thought to join up with the Taylor trail at track +2. Therefore, Taylor knew of 19 tracks in the "Taylor Trail" beyond +2, or through +21, ending with the cut-out, where Jacob McFall removed a print.

A comparison of photographs of the fresh prints when first excavated by Taylor and crew with the eroded, indistinct markings visible today underscores the need to uncover entirely new areas. Fields measures the average length at about 16 inches, while Taylor found that the best prints, the ones with no evidence of slippage, averaged about 10 inches. Erosion has taken a deadly toll.

As mentioned before, there are two dinosaur trails which intersect the Taylor Trail, one quite clear, and the other rather indistinct.

The direction of the trail is S 60° W.

Giant Run

This series of six large tracks is in a northerly direction. The tracks were made by an individual with a foot about 17" in length, while the print impressions

The lower portion of the Taylor Trail, as seen when first discovered. Facing page: The impoundment on the left in the aerial view is the lower Taylor site. Lower left print H-1; +1, lower right +2. This page: Upper left print H-1; +3. Upper right, +4. Lower left, +5. Lower right, +6. Compare these photos with the more recent photos below. © FFC, photos by P. Taylor.

The first three tracks in the "Giant Run." Next three tracks have been covered by bank debris.

are about 20" in length. Each print has concretions evident in the botom of the print, attesting to its authenticity. The average stride was about 55" from heel to heel. Stan Taylor asked a modern-day giant to try a cast of one of these on for size, and it fit fairly well. The clear dinosaur trail intersects the Giant Trail between prints one and two. Turnage and Taylor labeled this trail as H-2.

Giant Run Number	Length	Width	Depth	Stride to next print	Comments
H-2-1	18¾"	6"	1¾"	56"	Right
H-2-2	15¼"	8"	2-5/8"	34"	Left
H-2-3	23½"	11"	2½"	48"	Right edges broken
H-2-4	15¼"	7"	2¼"	39"	Left
H-2-5	20"	7"	5/8"	?	Right
H-2-6	-	-	-		Indistinct

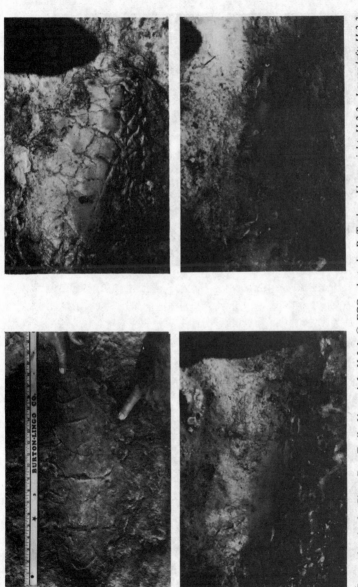

Four prints in the Giant Run Trail. Upper left: H-2-1, © FCC, photo by P. Taylor. Upper right: H-2-2. Lower left: H-2-3. Lower right: H-2-4, all photos by Henderson. The concretionary veins which can be seen in each print are secondary features and represent the filling in of mud cracks caused by the pressure from the foot. They are good evidence that the prints are not erosional features, and that they have not been overly altered.

The Turnage Trail, shown in upper left makes two direction changes. Upper right: The discovery of H-3-8. Lower left: H-3-7. and H-3-6. Lower right H-3-7.

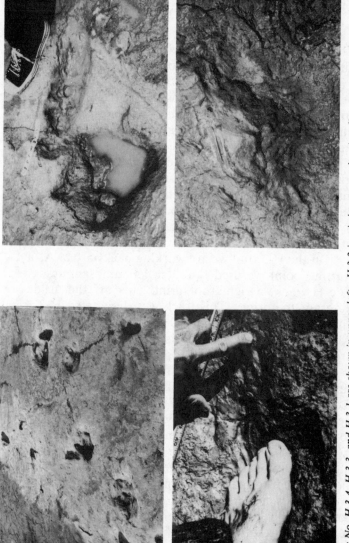

Prints No. H-3-4, H-3-3, and H-3-1 are shown in upper left. H-3-2 is missing or overlapping dinosaur print. Upper right: Print H-3-1 overlapping dinosaur print. Lower left: H-3-4. When print was made, the mud was slippery and toes grabbed to increase traction. Note scratch marks. Lower right: H-3-4.

Turnage Trail

In many ways this trail is the most human-like of all. The prints are not perfect specimens in that they show all the features of a human foot and have been passed over by numerous recent investigators. Turnage, Henderson, Ware, and crew, sponsored in part by the Institute for Creation Research, studied these prints much more intensively than any other trail has been studied, and the markings, once understood, provided a great deal of insight into the individual making the tracks, and the conditions under which they were made. The trail changes direction twice, but proceeds basically in a southerly direction. It was labeled H-3 by Turnage and Taylor. Mike Turnage's description of the trail follows:[7]

"On the H-3 trail we are working backwards. As a starting point we used D-R-3, a left dinosaur track. The H track, a right foot print, cuts off the inside dinosaur toe print. This track was designated H-3-1 and the trail intercepts the D-R trail on a diagonal. Although this track is somewhat eroded, some features are important.

"First, the forward part of the track where the toes sunk into the mud left five blunt impressions on the front-most part. The inside of the track is gouged out. Second, lateral scrape marks which could correspond to toenail marks gouged from the outside inward at two points. The possibility of these lateral marks being claws seems to be precluded by the blunt impressions in the front part of the track.

"H-3-2 is not evident. It either eroded away or could possibly have been made within the D-R-4 track. It would have been a left print.

"H-3-3, the right foot print was made by the same foot as H-3-1. From the toe area of H-3-1 to the toe area of H-3-3 is 7 feet. The media of the H-3-3 track involved slippage of the toes as did H-3-1.

"It appears that on both of these tracks, and the H-3-4 print, the toes were curled under and scrapes were made in the soft media to gain traction. This H-3-3 track slippage within the impression form what appears to be the toenail marks of the first, third, fourth, and fifth toes. In the heel area there is a swell in the rock caused by compression to the rear of the track as the toes dug in. Better definition is retained within this track than in the H-3-1 print. Length of the print is about 13½ inches. Width at the ball is about 6½ inches and heel width is about 3½ inches.

"H-3-4 represents a left foot print. It involves a double change in direction as the foot gouged to the rear within the print. On the front part of the track, slip marks are evident for the first, third, and fifth toes as they curled under for traction. After about an inch of reverse motion, slip marks begin approximately 25° to the left and involve the second, third, and fourth toes. These proceed for about 2 inches stopping abruptly in the heel area of the print. These three tracks, H-3-1, H-3-3, and H-3-4 all form a diagonal line that intercepts the dinosaur trail. H-3-5, a right foot print, is not evident.

"H-3-6 shows little definition. The media was more solid than in the three tracks just described. However, a few items are notable. The print is a left foot with compression to the outside of the track. A crease was evident between the big toe and ball of foot area. Direction of travel was changed from a perpendicular to a diagonal with the dinosaur trail after this print. This angle change was described within the H-3-4 track.

"All of the tracks described up to this point were excavated by Stanley Taylor in October, 1970. The next two described were first excavated in June, 1971.

"Track H-3-7 was the best in the trail. It showed the least erosion and best definition. Primarily, it clearly shows the instep side of a right human track. A depression for the big toe is indicated. A crease for the joint to the ball of the foot is present. The ball and arch of the instep are clearly shown. The media was limestone with a glossy gray shaley material within the print. Compression forced the then soft media forward and to the outside when the print was made. The mechanics of motion and angle from H-3-8 made this impression of the instep area plain. When compression occurred gray shaley media formed a V in front of the foot area.

"H-3-8, a left track, was made on more solid media and the track is not deep. The instep line is distinct and the foot area is outlined. From H-3-8 to H-3-7 there was a 30° change in direction of travel toward the left."

Ryals' Trail

In reality, Jim and Cecil Ryals discovered and removed human tracks from many trails, but this trail is rather well known and has come to be known as the Ryals Trail. It is in the middle of the river at the Taylor site.

Fields and company have proposed that the trail contains eight prints to go with the one hole where Ryals removed the print. Unfortunately, much of this trail is suspect. It is in an area where the river bottom is riddled with elongated ruts (tail drags or elongated joints). Several of the proposed prints are long and narrow, with few markings that would indicate human origin, and the evidence for continuity is subjective. However, the tracks immediately preceding and following the hole are quite good, and when first documented in the late 1960's, were unmistakable. Con-

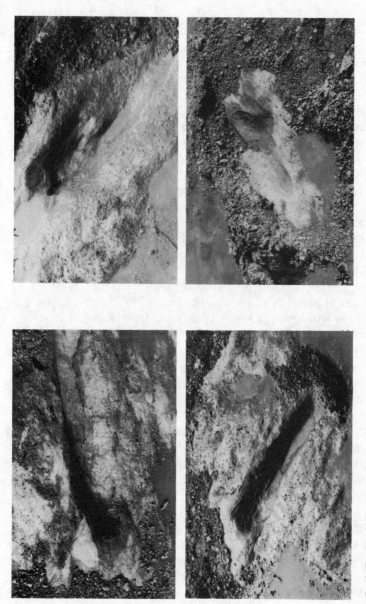

Ryals Trail in 1978. Upper left print No. Ry + 1. Upper right, Ry + 2. Lower left, Ry + 4. Lower right, Ry + 5. Ryals Hole is Ry + 3.

sequently, no claims are made for any of the other "prints," and this trail should be considered a series of only three prints, with one removed.

The preceding print, a right footprint (Ry +2) has a prominent indentation in the big toe area, perhaps made as the foot left the print. But clear toe markings representing the toe line protrude back under the surface. A reasonable stride for a person with such a large foot locates the hole where Ryals claims a left footprint was removed and sold to Dr. Cook in the 1930's. The same reasonable stride locates another right print (Ry +4) which is quite long compared to Ry +2, and may indicate that the walker slipped. The heel area of the final print may be in the approximate original location of the ball and toe of the foot before the slip took place.

The hole itself is also interesting. At the present time it is rather shallow, only about 5½'' deep. Some have wondered if such a thin slab of rock could have been removed intact. However, larger slabs of rock (with dinosaur prints) are known which are of the same thickness. The secret is in the way prints were removed. A circular trench around the print was cut by the hammer and chisel method, and then a circular iron band was placed around the print and tightened to give it strength. Next, the slab was torqued to break it loose from the underlying rock. It was important for transportation and handling purposes to keep the weight at a minimum, and this method worked, producing a thin, intact slab.

The following chart comes primarily from the work of Fields, Beierle, and crew in 1977 and 1978, revised to include the work of others. In 1977, Fields numbered the six known markings as Ry +1 to +6, and when in 1978 others were noted, they had to be labeled at Ry -1, -2, and -3. Keep in mind that all but prints

Ry + 2, + 3, and + 4 are in question.

Track No.	R/L	Lgth.	Width toe	Width heel	Depth	Stride	Comments
Ry -3	L?	14	5	3½	1	47	Indistinct and out of sequence with others. Has 3 faint toe-like impressions.
Ry -2	L	22	4½	-	-	47	Very shallow and indistinct. Suspect.
Ry -1	R	16	6	-	2	47	Does not have foot-like appearance. The bottom is curved, rather than flat.
Ry + 1	L	16	2	-	2	57	Very narrow.
Ry + 2	R	23	5	3½	3½	54	Has prominent big toe (1½" long. Faint toe ridge just below surface.
Ry + 3	L?	-	-	-	5½	54	45" x 29" oval shaped hole where track removed.
Ry + 4	R	29	5	4½	3	41	Unusually elongated. Foot may have slipped. Final position of heel near where toes had originally been. Toe scratches visible.
Ry + 5	L	18	3½	3	2	52	Elongated oval shaped depression.
Ry + 6	R	24	4½	3	1½		Shallow, but in series.

Caution is urged in using this evidence. As noted previously, "tail drags/joints" can appear as a right-left sequence, but the impressions give no indications of human origin, and the river here is full of these markings. Were it not for the testimony of Jim Ryals (in everyone's opinion, an honest and intelligent man) that he removed a clear track from this location, it is doubtful that these markings would receive much attention, other than prints + 2 and + 4.

Beierle Trail. The markings in this trail are of varied length and stride and are of uncertain origin.

Beierle Trail

During the extreme low-water conditions of the summer of 1978, Fred Beierle and family attempted to find the downstream extension of the Taylor Trail. Found was a series of markings that give some indication of being of human origin, others of being elongated ruts of uncertain origin. The markings have not been documented to any great detail, but certain features are worth commenting on. There are seven in left-right sequence with the eighth perhaps unrelated. All are about two inches deep.

Number	L/R	Estimated Length	Estimated stride to next print	Comments
1	L	15"	50"	Pointing in direction of print #2. Concave to inside. Unusual structure on outside.
2	R	18"	24"	Possible arch, possible toe scratches. Shallow channel at right angles to print to heel of print 3.
3	L	22"	50"	No clear toe area. Points in direction of print #4 and there is a shallow rut between them.
4	R	24"	26"	Has interesting markings in toe area. Very near heel of print #5.
5	L	30"	50"	Appears as a double print. Either elongated or foot slipped. Grades almost imperceptibly into print 6.
6	R	22"	-	Has pronounced indentations in toe area. Print direction is skewed to the outside from trail direction.
7	L	15"	-	One of three similar markings almost side by side.
8	R?	15"	-	Has an impression in the big toe area and interesting arch markings.

Without more investigation of this most inaccessible trail, it would not be wise to make the claim of human origin. This trail has some of the signs of our theoretical dinosaur tail drag, but could not be a simple joint structure since the trail is discontinuous. However, it should be noted that the long, short, long, short, long nature of the stride, and the fact that print 1 points to print 2, and 3 points to 4, and 5 points to 6, while between prints 2 and 3, and 4 and 5 the stride is rather short with a shallow rut between the toe of one and the heel of the next leads one to think of these as more "dinosaurian" than human.

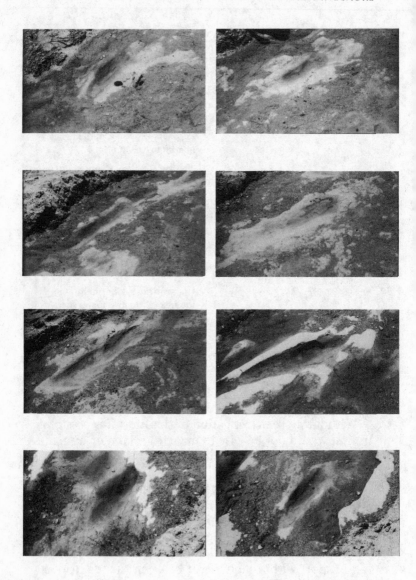

Prints in the Beierle Trail. Upper left B-1 through B-8 in lower right.

Point 11 (Turnage Site)

Mike Turnage, Tom Henderson, and crew attempted to establish the origin of a six-print series of manlike tracks by applying fingerprinting techniques to the prints. Of the six prints, the two nearest the center of the river were the best, but unfortunately, no "microprints" were evident. The center two were interesting and the last two were indefinite. Excavating back into the bank proved extremely difficult. The present west bank overlies the previous location of the river. The deposit here is loosely cemented sand and cobbles, but tightly packed. However, the farther back into the bank they proceeded the more the surface of the print layer deteriorated and broke off. Only the two indefinite prints were found with this endeavor. Since the identity of the prints could not be established with certainty, no firm claims were made, although the prints are better than some for which claims have been made.

The prints averaged 12 inches long and faint hints of toe impressions could be seen on the river end of the prints.

Point 12 (Dougherty Site)

Cecil Dougherty's main track, featured on numerous pages in his booklet[8] and elsewhere, including a reproduction in Eric von Daniken's latest book and movie venture, is a large impression 21 inches long and 9 inches wide, one side of which does resemble the instep of a right human foot. The outside of the print is poorly developed, and/or eroded down to the general elevation of the surrounding area. In fact, the next clear upwarp of rock, coupled with the "instep" would outline the general shape of a dinosaur track. In 1972, Mike Turnage and Tom Henderson inspected

Man-like track in Taylor trail studied by Turnage and Henderson.

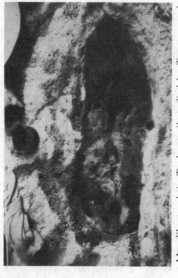

Mike Turnage and crew at work.

Mike Turnage used police detective techniques to see if possible human footprints had any "fingerprints." In below left he painted them with blue dye and below right he found no clear markings and abandoned trail.

The Dougherty print is 21½ inches long and 9 inches wide. Several less distinct tracks are also in this trail.

this print at length. Their conclusion that it was probably an eroded dinosaur print was based on the fact that the prominent big toe, which is separated from the next toe by a low ridge, is actually on the upswell of the impression, and not a deeper part as would be expected. The arch area is also wrong, being depressed from the surrounding print. Their most serious charge was that two of the toes appeared to have been recently etched into the rock by a metallic instrument.

In favor of the authenticity of the print, it should be noted that the previous inspection took place while the print was covered with shallow water. In addition, there are several similar, but less distinct markings leading up to Dougherty's print in a left right sequence with a relatively consistent stride. These prints are even less diagnostic than the main one, so that the origin of the print remains clouded in mystery.

The host shelf here is fairly smooth and could be

Cherry Trail. Note excellent toe markings. At Dougherty Site.

expected to contain accurate records. There is a very clear trail of 45 small dinosaur prints, so clear that on each left print, the middle toe shows that it had been deformed or shortened. This has led some to call it the "stubby" dinosaur trail. The eleventh track in this northward trail is only 8 inches from the Dougherty print.

In the same shelf are more easily recognizable prints. Miss Cherry May discovered the three-print Cherry trail in 1975. The prints are about 9 inches long, and while shallow, are in the exact shape of a human foot.

Perhaps the most perfect human footprint ever photographed in the river bed is just a few feet away from the Dougherty print, located near the 1½ foot ledge of the marker bed which forms a waterfall in the middle of the river. The print measures 13 inches long and 4 inches wide. This right print showed distinct toe markings of all five toes. A close look revealed that the print was probably made while standing instead of walking, for toe impressions had been moved about ½ inch from their original position. Near the heel of the print was another similar but smaller right foot print.

The prints had been recently exposed by a breaking of the overlying ledge and erosion of the intervening clay layer. Unfortunately, the mechanisms which exposed the prints had been responsible for the near-complete erosion of the previous ones and the falling water, which landed directly on the new prints, eroded them almost beyond recognition in nine months time. The succeeding prints would be still under the ledge, and if further chunks break off, it would be worthwhile to look for them.

There are numerous markings of almost any conceivable shape between the Dougherty site and the fourth crossing. During dry seasons, it might prove profitable to investigate this.

The "Morris" print, as it has come to be known, was found by the author in 1975. Within 9 months it had almost completely eroded, even though when first discovered it was perhaps the most perfect print ever photographed.

Point 21 (Park Ledge)

Visitors to the Dinosaur Valley State Park must cross the river via a series of stepping stones to see the most popular footprint locations. Clearly marked are two brontosaur prints and several different types of three-toed prints. But on an overlying ledge, about 3 feet above the main print layer are numerous man-like impressions, two bear-like impressions, and two badly deformed brontosaur-like markings.

The human prints are not immediately obvious to the casual observer, although they are almost always in plain sight. Standing in the more downstream of the two brontosaur tracks, three of the tracks on the upper ledge can be reached. These three tracks are part of two separate trails which converge slightly and intersect near the brontosaur tracks. All three are of rather poor detail.

Two of these prints are evidently part of a trail of five prints with two more expected prints missing. All five had previously been marked with yellow paint on each side of each print, but only faint patches remain. The direction of progress was S-20°-E, heading basically upstream. The first of the series is about 15 feet from the ledge border. It is about 13 inches long and shows that the foot slipped as the print was made. It is definitely a left footprint with interesting toe markings. The next print is evidently missing, and 7 feet from the first is another left print with all five toes visible. The second toe is slightly longer than the big toe, but both made good impressions. It is about 13 inches long as is the next print, a right print, 50 inches away. It too has all the toes visible, with good toe separation between the big and second toes. By extending the line made by these three prints, the final two are found (within reach of the brontosaur track). They

Park Ledge. *Upper left: View along the trail of 5 man-like tracks. Upper right: Prominent toe structure in second of 5 prints. Lower left: Bear-like track. Lower right: Possible combination of 2 or 3 man-like prints near eroded brontosaur print. Upper and lower right* FFC, *by P. Taylor.*

are separated by 12 feet from the third track, but appear to be in the same trail. The fourth is a right foot, and although wider than the others, is about the same length. The last is a left print about 14 inches long, making the composite trail L,-,L,R,-,R,L.

The other print within reach of the brontosaur is about 3½ feet from the edge. This track is thought by some to be the second in a series of two tracks which trend in the direction S-10°-E converging slightly with the trail described above. This print lacks detail, but the deepest impression is where the big toe of a left foot would be. The whole track is smooth and depressed about 2 inches below the surrounding ledge. It is compatible in size and general contour with the first in the supposed series, some 19 feet, 2 inches away. It is also a left print which measure 16 inches long and 7½ inches wide and has the precise contour of a large human foot. The heel mark shows clearly where the heel entered the mud, slid slightly forward and came to rest. The contour about the toes is clear although individual toes are not registered. The arch area has been fractured and somewhat eroded. The print can be seen only 15 inches from the edge of the ledge.

The writer feels it is somewhat presumptuous to assert that these two prints, while each shows evidence of human origin, are part of a single trail, separated as they are by 19 feet. Three interval tracks would make the average stride 58 inches long, reasonable in light of the size of the print, but too much guesswork is involved.

A third trail of three prints with none missing lies between the "series" of two and the series of five prints. It trends in very nearly a southerly direction and should have intersected the series of five at about the third print. The prints are all fairly shallow and

Various prints and trails of possible human footprints found on the Park Ledge. Upper left: Mrs. Marian Taylor points out two human trails, prints in standing position behind and to her left. Upper right: Well-formed human-like footprint. Lower left: Very good toe impressions preserved. Lower right: Possible brontosaur print and three possible human prints. Photo upper right by Burdick; remainder © FFC by P. Taylor.

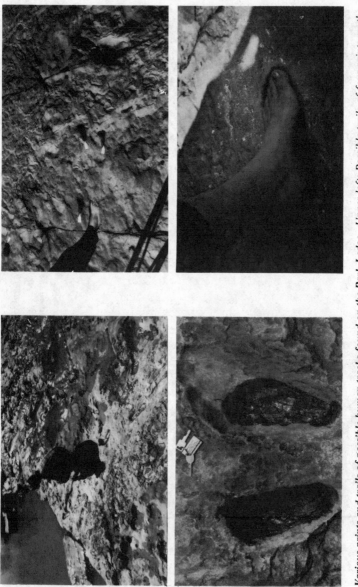

Various prints and trails of possible human tracks found on the Park Ledge. Upper left: *Possible trails of four prints on the north end of the ledge.* Upper right: *Possible footprints of a child, approximately 5½" long.* Lower left: *Two prints, seemingly in a standing position.* Lower right: *Deeply impressed possible human track.* © *FFC photos by P. Taylor, except lower left.*

are on the order of 10 inches long and 3 inches wide. The first of the three shows definite toe impressions and all three are consistent in size and direction.

The clearest of the two bear-like impressions is about 32 feet from the southerly end of the ledge and 10 feet west of the brontosaur track. It is distinct in contour, measuring 14 inches by 8 inches, pointing northward. All four claw marks are clearly imprinted. It has not been conclusively shown to be a bear, but almost certainly represents a large mammal. The other bear-like print is on the north end of the ledge, near the end of the stepping stone bridge, but it is much less clear, and the two are not in series.

A four-track trail of possible prints can be seen between the clear "bear" track and the south end of the ledge. Three tracks can be seen near the eroded brontosaur track near the center of the ledge.

Numerous other markings have been noted on the ledge, many in the shape of a human foot. Ranging from 5 inches to 16 inches, these prints are not in any series at all. Two prints are found together, of the same size and shape (one right and one left) in a standing position, as if a human were standing with feet slightly skewed apart.

All of the prints have eroded significantly in the last decade, as multiplied thousands have tromped across the ledge.

Point 24 (Burdick Trail)

Dr. Burdick found this trail years ago. It was extended into the bank by Burdick, Taylor, and volunteer workers. As Westcott writes:[9]

"[The trail] . . . is off the east side of the plain area after the river has turned and flows south. Here two humanoid tracks are found in the stream bed near the west bank. The first is 7 feet out from the sandy bank,

Point 24, Burdick Trail. Digging into the bank revealed this marking, which is obviously not an erosional feature. It is in a regular stride with two other similar tracks, which seem to have been made by a human-like foot wrapped with a protective covering.

while the second is at the bank itself. A third track is located six feet into the bank and was exposed for study in 1968. All are imprinted in a hard, level limestone stratum 6 inches below water level. The orientation is westward and the stride measured heel to heel is 70 inches. The track itself has a contour compatible with that of a large human foot, and is about 16 inches long. The heel is readily distinguished as it slid forward into the mud as the foot descended to an exceptional depth of some 6 inches. This depth, coupled with a 6-foot stride, probably represents a running gait in what was soft mud.

"Forty inches south of the first track and also 7 feet out from the bank lies a perfect print of a three-toed saurian. It is at exactly the same level in the same stratum. Its depth is 3 inches and its length 17 inches. Some 10 feet north or upstream to the humanoid tracks are other similar saurian tracks of excellent quality, also in the same stratum.''

Point 28 (Shakey Springs)

This is the site of the unusual elongated dinosaur trails, which could easily be misinterpreted. It is recommended that investigators thoroughly familiarize themselves with these trails and the similar trail at the McFall site before studying and searching for others.

Point 29 (Mack Farm)

Upstream from the second crossing are numerous elongated markings, parallel to the river flow, and lacking any precise detail. These should not be used as evidence.

Point 35. Between the bridge and the dam in Glen Rose are several faint markings which appear as man-prints to Dr. Dougherty. This author remains unconvinced. The "prints" shown here are greased for clarity. Photo by Dougherty.

Point 35 (Dam in Glen Rose)

Three shallow and subjective markings in the print layer are not of sufficient detail to allow a precise diagnosis.

At times other man-like markings have been discovered in the Glen Rose Limestone in other areas where the layer is exposed.

Prints have been reported on the Hondo Creek near Bandera, Texas, which upon closer examination proved to be classic cases of eroded mid-river joints appearing as a trail of elongated prints very near clear dinosaur tracks. Similar discoveries in the Blanco Creek, Guadalupe River, Cowhouse Creek, the Middle Verde Creek, and Sabinal River, have likewise been reinterpreted by further study.

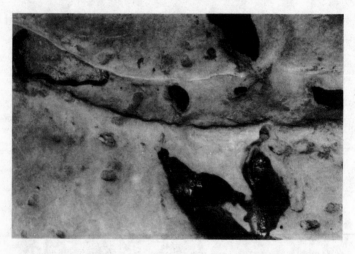

A possible "tail-drag" in the Bosque River near Iredel, Texas, has a 1" thick wooden "plank" embedded in Limestone which shows up where erosion has exposed it. Note nearby dinosaur tracks. Photo by DiPietro.

Marvin Herrmann of Films for Christ found this possible man track in the Bosque River bed. Photo by Herrmann.

Other reports still lack complete documentation. In 1936 Bull Adams found a series of five "wrapped" tracks which led back under the bank of the Rock Creek south of Glen Rose. In 1970 Slim Adams showed several investigators, including the author, the location of the prints, but at the time the prints were covered with rubble. He remembers the series traveling in a southeasterly direction, with 10-inch prints so clear that even the stitching on the foot covering was visible, including a place where the stitching was broken, and a dangling leather thong or flap was seen in every other print.

The dry conditions of 1978 also exposed dinosaur

tracks in the Bosque near Iredell, Texas, south of Glen Rose. Investigator Walter DiPietro writes:

"I was impressed with the quantity of the tracks, often appearing to be heading in no apparent direction. Nonetheless, their quality was inferior to the Paluxy tracks. Man tracks were also alleged to be present, though these required some imagination. The best found was a set of four tracks, elongated, shallow, and containing wrinkles where one would suspect the toes to be found.

"Of equal or greater significance was the discovery of a plank of black carbonized word that was exposed by a "tail drag." The wood was exactly like one would expect a handworked piece of wood to appear. But what was this ancient wooden plank still embedded in the solid rock substrata doing here?"[10]

Marvin Herrman, of Films for Christ also happened to be in Texas when news of the Iredell prints reached him. He was able to find several shallow prints shaped like human feet, but they were not of sufficient quality to conclude a human origin.

Reference for the Appendix

1. Taylor, Stanley A., "Search for Man Tracks in the Paluxy River," Special Report, Films for Christ, October, 1968.
2. Ware, James, (unpublished summary), June, 1971.
3. Westcott, George W., "Fossil Tracks in the Paluxy River Beds," (unpublished manuscript), pp. 5, 6.
4. *Ibid.*
5. Taylor
6. Fields, Wilbur, "Paluxy River Exploration: 1977-78," Jopin, Missouri, 1978.
7. Turnage, Mike, (unpublished report to ICR), 1971, pp. 2, 3.
8. Dougherty, Cecil, *Valley of the Giants,* 6th ed., Glen Rose, Texas, 1980.
9. Westcott, pp. 14-17.
10. DiPietro, Walter, personal correspondence, March, 1979.

Credits

Marvin Ross—illustrations

Paul Anderson—photography re-worked

John Morris—initial photography

Paul Taylor, Marvin Herrman, Cecil Dougherty, Walter DiPietro, Clifford Burdick, Wilbur Fields, Peter Jones, Charlie Moss, Slim Adams, Louise Berry, and the U.S. Geologic Survey all provided photographs included in this book.